FORCE OF NATURE

BY STEVEN DIETZ

Based on Goethe's *Elective Affinities*

★

★

DRAMATISTS
PLAY SERVICE
INC.

for Joe Hanreddy

AUTHOR'S NOTE

DESTINY: SOME THOUGHTS ON *FORCE OF NATURE*

Man supposes that he directs his life and governs his actions,
when his existence is irretrievably under the control of destiny.
                                                            —Goethe

Imagine the outrage. Imagine the look on your face. Imagine the fallout if your spouse, or close friend, or co-worker looked you in the eye and said, with no hint of apology: "Yes, it's true. I have fallen madly and completely in love with someone new. I know my life will be irrevocably changed from this moment on, but I will not fear the consequences, for this is the love I was destined to find." You say you want the truth from people. Oh, *really?* Just how much truth would you like? "Pardon me, honey, but I think that woman at the bar is my Destiny. I'll be in touch."

We live in a noisy world. The chemically-bonded notions of love and attraction are everywhere — selling us perfume, beer and minivans, filling the airwaves with fodder for our true national pastime: rampant public confession. The "free love" generation has devolved into the society of "free guilt." Grace is cheap and redemption assured. Never have so many confessed so much about so little.

How odd, then, that as the culture grows more lurid ... our own hearts seem to grow timid. We increasingly mistrust what Goethe calls "the substantial event" — the all-consuming power of love's passion — for we know it will crush our common defenses of irony, avoidance and complaint. We listen to reason, and reason — in matters of passion — makes cowards of us all. We don't have *time* to fall in love (again). We have things to *do*. And what's more: "What would people *say?*" Over time, we become incrementalists of the heart. In emotional matters, we content ourselves with taking tiny steps in the direction of commitment or departure, hoping our battery of hints and slights will some day accumulate into a groundswell of action. We demand less. We modify our hopes. We get by on greeting cards and gossip. This emotional relativism helps us to make do with the crumbs from love's table; it allows us to accept the fallacy that "big love" happens only to other people, only in the movies.

But, still, our hearts know differently.

In Goethe's odd and remarkable novella *Elective Affinities*, he places his four central characters in the very heart of love's storm. He denies them the chance to avoid or minimize the call of their hearts — forcing them to either grow brave or perish. Here, then, in a one hundred and ninety year-old novel is the subtext of our own lives. Here is a story about what churns beneath our world of surface intimacy, witty comebacks and wished-for Hollywood endings. Here is what happens when the "substantial event" is not only unleashed — but embraced.

> *That is the true season of love, when we believe that we alone can love, that no one could ever have loved so before us, and that no one will love in the same way after us.*
> —*Goethe*

Imagine the outrage. Imagine what people will say.

—*Steven Dietz*
19 March '99
Santa Monica, CA

FORCE OF NATURE was commissioned and originally produced by the Milwaukee Repertory Theater (Joseph Hanreddy, Artistic Director; Timothy J. Shields, Managing Director) in Milwaukee, Wisconsin, on April 9, 1999. It was directed by Joseph Hanreddy; the set and lighting design were by Kent Dorsey; the sound design was by Michael Bodeen and Rob Milburn; the costume design was by Laura Crow; and the stage manager was Judy Berdan. The cast was as follows:

ED / EDWARD .... Andrew May
CHARLOTTE .... Laura Gordon
CAP / THE CAPTAIN .... James Pickering
OTTILIE .... Kirsten Potter
CURT / THE COUNT .... Peter Silbert
SHARON / THE BARONESS .... Rose Pickering
NICK / NICOLAS .... Brian Vaughn
LUCY / LUCIANNE .... Deborah Staples
MITTLER .... Lee E. Ernst
YOUNG WOMAN .... Melissa Cannaday
THE HUSBAND .... Jeremy Woods

FORCE OF NATURE was subsequently produced by the Oregon Shakespeare Festival (Libby Appel, Artistic Director; Paul Nicholson, Executive Director) in Ashland, Oregon, on April 22, 2000. It was directed by James Edmondson; the set design was by Richard L. Hay; the lighting design was by Robert Peterson; the sound design was by Todd Barton; the costume design was by Galina Solovyeva; the dramaturgy was by Douglas Langworthy; and the stage manager was David W. Wieken. The cast was as follows:

ED / EDWARD .... Michael Elich
CHARLOTTE .... Robin Goodrin Nordli
CAP / THE CAPTAIN .... Richard Elmore
OTTILIE .... Bridgette Loriaux
CURT / THE COUNT .... Jeffrey King
SHARON / THE BARONESS .... Linda Alper
NICK / NICOLAS .... John Hansen
MITTLER .... Linda Morris
YOUNG WOMAN .... Tony DeBruno
MUSICIANS .... Daniel Flick
Jennifer Perry

CHARACTERS
(5 men, 4 women, doubling as indicated)

ED / EDWARD — a wealthy nobleman in his late thirties

CHARLOTTE — Edward's wife, also in her late thirties

CAP / THE CAPTAIN — a former soldier, Edward's friend, fifties

OTTILIE — a young woman, twenty

CURT / THE COUNT* — a nobleman, forties

THE HUSBAND — a jealous man, French

SHARON / THE BARONESS — a noblewoman, also in her forties

NICK / NICOLAS — a schoolmaster, late twenties

LUCY / LUCIANNE** — Charlotte's niece, twenty

THE YOUNG WOMAN — a vision

MITTLER — a very busy man in his forties

TIME and PLACE

The present. A park.
1809. An estate in the German countryside.

SETTING

A large open playing space which will be transformed into a variety of locales. Small pieces brought on, as noted. Simple and elegant. The ability to move fluidly from one scene to the next — without blackouts — is fundamental to the rhythm of the play.

MUSIC

Unless otherwise noted, all musical compositions are by Franz Schubert.

* Actor playing CURT / THE COUNT doubles as THE HUSBAND.
** Actress playing LUCY / LUCIANNE doubles as THE YOUNG WOMAN.

SUGGESTED MUSIC

All of the following compositions are by Franz Schubert:

MAIN THEME [MAJOR]
Polonaise for Violin and Chamber Orchestra, [D. 580].

MAIN THEME [MINOR]
First movement of the Sonata for Cello and Piano in A minor, "Arpeggione" [D. 821].

OTTILIE
Variation on a Waltz by Diabelli, [D. 718].

EDWARD
The Andante movement of the Sonatina in G minor, [D. 408].

THE CAPTAIN
First movement of the Sonatina in D Major, [D. 384].

EDWARD AND OTTILIE
"Nacht und Träume" from *Lieder*, [D. 827].

CHARLOTTE AND THE CAPTAIN
First movement of the Duo in A Major, [D. 574].

MITTLER
Moderato in C-sharp minor, from "6 Moments Musicuax," [D. 78].

NICOLAS
The Trio movement in B-flat for Violin, Viola and Cello, [D. 471].

FIREWORKS
"Nahe des Geliebten" from *Lieder*, [D. 162].

THE DUEL
"Das Wirtshaus" from *Winterreise*, [D. 911].

THE STORM
The Violin Sonata in D, [D.384] — at approx. 1:20.

THE CHILD
Impromptu No. 3 in B-flat, [D. 935].

CELEBRATION/CHRISTENING OF PAVILION
Konzertstück for Violin and Orchestra in D, [D. 345].

"To Duty much, to Love far more we owe."
—Goethe, *The Diary*

FORCE OF NATURE

PROLOGUE

A shaft of light rises on Ed. He speaks in a friendly, familiar way to the audience.

ED. I would tell you a story, but you wouldn't believe me. I would give you reasons enough to see yourself in my place, but you would not be persuaded. And perhaps that is wise. *(As he continues, he lifts a book — and we realize that he is reading these words.)* Because to accept this fate — as I did — to throw open the doors of your life to something you could not have imagined and cannot control ... that is dangerous. And terrifying. And unforgettable. *(Music [Schubert] plays, as a shaft of moonlight reveals —)*

An Upper Window. Night.

(Framed in the window — beautifully and memorably — is a woman's unclothed back, simple and alluring. This is Ottilie.) "It is about a moment. A moment that shakes you to the quick. And after that moment has vanished ... *(The image of Ottilie slowly fades away, as the music, too, fades away, and Ed closes the book.)* ... you will do anything — *everything* — to win it back once again."

A Park. The Present. Day.

Bright sunshine begins to flood the stage, as music [contemporary, driving beat] is heard, distantly, coming from an off-stage boom box. A Frisbee flies on and lands at center, near Ed, followed by Lucy and Nick. They are chasing/wrestling with/seducing one another. Lucy carries several picnic blankets. Nick carries the boom box, which continues to play, until noted.

Note on clothing: Everyone in the following scene is dressed in light, casual, predominantly white clothing. A sense of air and light; carefree pleasure.

LUCY. I get to choose!
NICK. *(Laughing.)* No, Lucy, I don't think you —
LUCY. Yes, I get to choose the spot. Aunt Charlotte told me I could, and I think — *(Looking around.)* here. (Lucy drops the blanket and turns to Nick. Without hesitation, she takes his face in her hands and kisses him long and hard on the mouth. In one instant, the playfulness gives way to passion. Nick drops the boom box, though it continues to play.)*
NICK. Yes.
LUCY. Right … here. *(They fall back upon the still-folded blankets, their bodies intertwined, as Charlotte enters, arm in arm with Cap. Charlotte carries a picnic basket. Cap has a backpack slung over his shoulder, and is carrying a small cooler. Lucy and Nick are unaware of them.)*
CHARLOTTE. *(As they enter.)* But that's the thing: Marriage is not a *sacrament* — it's a *work of art*. And like any work of art, we no more know the reason it *succeeds* than the reason it *fails*. *(They stop when they see Lucy and Nick on the ground. They look across the stage to Ed.)*
CAP. What was it we *called* that? Back when we all used to *do* that?
ED. Lust.
CAP. Right. *(Smiling, they watch Lucy and Nick go at it.)*

ED. When did Lucy meet him?

CHARLOTTE. Last night, I think.

CAP. It seems to be going very well. *(Charlotte and Cap set their things down, as Ed goes to the boom box and turns it off. When he does Lucy and Nick suddenly look up at him.)*

LUCY. Hello, Uncle. This is Nick.

ED. Hi, Nick.

NICK. Great day for a picnic! What are you reading? *(Ed hands the book to Nick, as Charlotte says —)*

CHARLOTTE. *(To Cap.)* It's the book I bought him. He can't put it down.

CAP. Really? What is it, Ed?

ED. *(With a laugh.)* It's nothing. *(Ed busies himself with readying the picnic, as —)*

CHARLOTTE. My husband does not share my belief in *Destiny.*

ED. Oh, please don't start —

CHARLOTTE. I've always believed that there is one person in the world whom we are destined to find. Call it what you will — a true love, a soul mate — I believe that for each of us that one person exists.

CAP. *(With a smile.)* There's hope for me still.

CHARLOTTE. And I found a book which makes my point.

CAP. So, what's the word, Ed?

ED. *(Handing the book to Nick.)* As something to read on the plane or in the bathroom, it's not bad.

CHARLOTTE. *(To Cap, enjoying herself.)* Till two A.M. last night, pouring over it in bed — *(Lucy goes quickly to Charlotte, as Nick moves away and reads the book, and Ed looks into the distance.)*

ED. Didn't there used to be a row of poplars over there?

LUCY. Do you like Nick? Isn't he handsome?

CHARLOTTE. Well, yes, he seems to be a —

LUCY. And you know what else? *(Moves closer to Charlotte.)* He had his heart broken. Just a few months ago. This grad student he was seeing — she was all "I really love you" and "Let's be together always" and then BAM: over. *(Whispers, with awe.)* He was *devastated.* *(Beat.)* I love that. I always wanted to meet someone who'd had their heart broken. Not, you know, "*pretend*-broken" — not like "he promised to call me and he didn't" — but the *real deal,* with lots of sobbing and screaming and deeply important thoughts filled with bitterness and angst. You know, like in *books*. *(Charlotte just stares at her.)* What's to drink? *(Lucy goes immediately to the cooler, as Mittler enters, carrying a camera on a tripod.)*

MITTLER. Oh, Charlotte, I love this park! *(Calling to them as he enters.)* Hello, Ed — Hello, Cap — *(Ed waves. Cap nods.)*

LUCY. *(Looking up from the cooler.)* Hello, Mister Mittler!

MITTLER. What a day! You know something, Charlotte, this park always makes me think of your wedding. We did the photos right up against that row of — *(Stops.)* Where did the trees go?

ED. You remember them, too.

CAP. They were cut down as part of the re-design.

MITTLER. The what?

CAP. *(Pointing into the distance.)* They're taking out those trees and diverting the stream to the west. Putting in a gazebo and more parking.

MITTLER. Why don't they try *leaving well enough alone*?! Nature, after all, is not man's *plaything*, it is a —

CAP. Well, in fact, that's *exactly* what it is. To whom does Nature belong if not to man?

MITTLER. Oh, here we go! All bow to the ground: the expert is speaking!

CAP. *(Furious, overlapping from "ground")* If you'd only listen to —

CHARLOTTE. *Enough. (A smile.)* Now, boys. We're usually able to make it through the chips and dip before you go at each other's throats.

MITTLER. But, Charlotte —

CHARLOTTE. So, please: *a truce.*

NICK. *(Looking up from the book.)* More parking would be good. More parking is always good. *(Everyone looks at Nick for a beat, then they decide to ignore his remark and return to the picnic. Mittler gets something to drink from the cooler and prepares his camera for a photo. Cap and Ed begin tossing the Frisbee. Charlotte opens the picnic basket, as Lucy takes the final things out of the backpack.)*

LUCY. Aunt Charlotte?

CHARLOTTE. Hmm?

LUCY. What's this? *(Lucy removes a small wooden box from the backpack. Charlotte opens the box as she speaks.)*

CHARLOTTE. Sentiment. Superstition maybe. *(Charlotte removes a simple glass chalice from the box and holds it up in the sunlight. Of the others, only Ed turns and watches her do this.)* It's our wedding chalice. The first time we drank from it was in this park, years ago. So, rather than pack it away, or lock it up behind glass, once a year I bring it with us. *(Charlotte hands the chalice to Lucy, who looks at it with unabashed reverence.)*

LUCY. I want to get some rituals. Can you tell me how? Everything I do is so, you know, *disposable* — I want to start having traditions and rituals and things that — when I do them — mean *more* than just what they *look like.* You know?

ED. How's business, Mittler?

MITTLER. Hey, marriages are "cool" again. And thank god for that. The seventies almost killed me. But now everybody's tying the knot and they all want their picture taken.

ED. And what about you? You were seeing that woman — I can't think of her name —

CHARLOTTE. Evonne.

ED. Yes. Evonne.

MITTLER. We had a falling out.

CHARLOTTE.	LUCY.
Sorry to hear that.	Oh, no …

MITTLER. New Year's Eve she looks at me and says: "Honey, I think we need to talk."

ED.	CAP.	NICK.
Bad sign.	Uh-oh.	Run for your life.

MITTLER. And while she sat across from me talking about "commitment" and "the future," I thought about the thousand weddings I have shot in my life. And every time I click the shutter I think to myself: There. I will print that. And it will be framed and hung on a wall. And chances are that frozen, idyllic image will be the *one part of this marriage that will last.*

CHARLOTTE. You've become such a cynic.

MITTLER. At least I've tried to be in love. *(To Cap.)* Some of us have never even done that.

ED.	CHARLOTTE.
Mittler —	Oh, please —

MITTLER. I think the last time Cap brought a woman to this

picnic was when his mother was in town.

CAP. And she didn't think much of *you.*

CHARLOTTE. *(To Mittler.)* Cap is a confirmed bachelor and you know it.

CAP. That's not true. I am an *unconfirmed bachelor.* As you were saying, Charlotte, I have never found that *one person* — the person I was destined to be with.

LUCY. That's so *sad.*

CHARLOTTE. Do you hear this, Ed? Even your best friend believes what's in that book.

MITTLER. *(To Ed.)* You don't think such a person exists?

ED. *(Not defensively.)* Yes, I do, and her name is Charlotte and I cherish her more today than the day I married her. So, the thought that somewhere in the world there is a woman who is not just my love, but my *Destiny* is not only foolhardy — it's beside the point.

NICK. But it's out of your control. *(All turn to Nick.)*

ED. Pardon me?

NICK. I wrote a paper on this. You can't just *decide* that someone new will not disrupt your life. Either it will happen or it won't.

ED. But I'm sure it won't.

MITTLER. You can't imagine meeting someone who would make you question your marriage?

ED. *(The truth.)* No, I can't.

CHARLOTTE. I can. *(They all look at her.)*

ED. Oh, really?

CHARLOTTE. Absolutely. I don't want to — it wouldn't be pleasant or convenient — and I'd like to think I'd choose to stay with Ed, whom I love and adore —

ED. Thank you so much.

CHARLOTTE. In *theory* — *yes,* I have to believe that a surprise like that waits for each of us, hovering somewhere in the world. *(Curt and Sharon enter, wearing sunglasses. Sharon carries a lovely white parasol. Curt carries a few badminton rackets and a bottle of champagne, unopened. They give the impression of having a delicious secret.)*

SHARON.	CURT.	OTHERS.
Hello, friends.	Good day, good day.	*(General greetings.)*

CHARLOTTE. I was starting to worry about you.

SHARON. Oh, the phone rang just as we were leaving. It was Ottilie *(Oh-TEEL-ya.)* — our young friend who we'd hoped to bring with us.

LUCY. *Ott-i-lie.* What kind of name is that?

CURT. She very much wanted to meet all of you — but something's come up.

SHARON. Something with her car, or something —

CURT. We're not sure, really — she can be very hard to read —

SHARON. Which is a young woman's gift. Our sense of mystery seems to vanish as we age.

CURT. *(With a smile.)* Not so, dear. I still find you impossible to read.

SHARON. I told Ottilie we'd be here all day and to stop by later if she could.

CURT. Which I'm sure she will.

CHARLOTTE. I'd love to meet her. *(Silence, then a burst of activity.)* Well, I hope you're hungry. Lucy and I were just unpacking the — *(— and simultaneous conversations —)*

CAP.	NICK	SHARON.
You look good, Curt.	I'm starving.	Curt brought chips.
CURT.	LUCY.	CHARLOTTE.
Well, I've been —	My aunt's a great —	So, tell me, what's —

MITTLER. *(Interrupting them all.)* Excuse me. *(They turn to Mittler.)* I think we've forgotten something.

CAP. Oh, god help us. *(Mittler puts them in place for a photo, as he speaks. The others sigh and emit a certain amount of good-natured grumbling — except for Lucy, who combs out her long hair and readies herself with enthusiasm.)*

MITTLER. Grumble all you want, but remember this: in a world that is too busy and noisy by half, the allure of a photo is that it offers both *permanence* and *reflection.*

NICK. Does he always talk like this?

CAP. Just when he's awake.

MITTLER. Only the photographer can show us that fundamental part of our nature which constantly and placidly endures. *(They are now positioned to Mittler's satisfaction.)* Very good. Now, don't move. *(Mittler goes to the camera and focuses/readies it.)*

CAP. Your friend, Ottilie, who is she?

SHARON. We met her on our trip to Europe. Curt was terribly smitten with her.

CURT. Guilty as charged.

SHARON. So bright and full of promise that I wanted to strangle her — but then I, too, fell under her spell.

CURT. *(Teasingly, to the men.)* Oh, if I were not so happily married —

EDWARD. *(Still stuck on an earlier topic.)* You see! It's too easy to walk away.

CAP. *(With a laugh.)* Let it go, Ed.

ED. When it comes to marriage, it should be at least as hard to *leave* as it is to *stay*.

CURT. I've always thought marriages should be granted in five year renewable increments.

CHARLOTTE. And after five years — what then?

CURT. You either part company —

SHARON. Or sign up for another tour of duty.

CAP. Just like the army.

LUCY. That's not very romantic.

MITTLER. I need everyone looking right here.

NICK. Love has nothing to do with it — it's all about chemicals.

LUCY.	CURT.	CAP.
What do you mean?	How's that?	He's got a point.

NICK. The cells of the body regenerate every seven years — so whoever you married back then is a *complete stranger* to you now. *(Ad-libs/laughter.)*

CHARLOTTE. Is that so?

NICK. I wrote a paper on this.

MITTLER. Okay. Here we *go. (Mittler pushes a button, then quickly moves and takes his place in the photo. There is a final bit of horseplay and ad-libs, including —)*

CURT. Oh, I think I left the car running — *(Sharon grabs Curt as he pretends to start off, the others sharing in the laugh, then — A moment of stillness is achieved ... a truly lovely, memorable picture is realized, as — the amplified click of a camera echoes through the theatre, and lights immediately replicate the photo — isolating the gathering of friends, who remain frozen in position. Silence, then ...)*

ACT ONE

... Ed turns his head and looks at the others. They do not move. Ed slowly "steps out of the photo" and moves away, looking back at the others. Taking in the picture. He turns and looks at the audience. Then, he walks over to where he left his book. Retrieves it. Starts back toward the audience, then stops — seeing the boom box. He presses a button on the boom box and — music [Schubert] plays softly, under. Ed steps downstage into a shaft of light, separate from the others, looking at the audience. As he opens the book ... The light on the photo slowly fades away and is gone. Ed, who will now be known as Edward, reads to the audience, buoyantly —

EDWARD. "Edward was the name of a nobleman in the prime of his life. And on this, the loveliest day of the year, he stood high on a hill which overlooked his estate. *(Looking up from the book, into the distance.)* His wife of many years, Charlotte, had just completed her latest project: a park, newly landscaped, with a stream which wound between the trees. On this day, as he stood viewing the vista of his own life, he was overwhelmed by one clear and powerful thought — "

A Hillside, Overlooking a German Country Estate. Day. The Year is 1809.

Music fades, and lights expand, as Charlotte steps forward, now wearing a portion of her period costume, circa 1809, over her contemporary clothing. She carries with her a coat of Edward's from the same period.

CHARLOTTE. What do you see?

EDWARD. *(Turning to her.)* Hmm?

CHARLOTTE. When you stare so long at your estate, what do you see?

EDWARD. A life which is complete. *(As Charlotte helps him on with his coat.)* When I think of the years I traveled hither and yon in search of That Which Was Missing — and for *what*?! I wasted my youth trying to attain, prematurely, the very things which came naturally with age.

CHARLOTTE. And those were?

EDWARD. *(His simple answer surprises even him.)* You. A longer list is available at your request, but the fundamental answer is: *you.* *(He tenderly touches her cheek. Holding one another, they look out at the vista before them.)*

CHARLOTTE. You haven't told me what you think of the park. I so hoped you would find it appealing. *(Pause.)* But you don't.

EDWARD. No, I don't.

CHARLOTTE. I see.

EDWARD. I find it to be … *glorious.* It does, of course, have great appeal, but the very word — like "youth" or "summer" — implies *transience* … *(Looking at the land below.)* … and, there is no transience here. You have, Charlotte — with your heart and mind and hands — made something glorious and eternal. Something that will outlast us all. *(Charlotte smiles and turns to the audience. Note: The tone of each "aside" to the audience is one of familiarity and candor.)*

CHARLOTTE. *(Aside.)* We fell in love the moment we met.

24

Unfortunately, our families had already married us off to partners we deplored. My husband was a soldier. Edward's wife was an older noblewoman. Upon her death, Edward traveled alone ... all over the world ... as I stood trapped in a loveless marriage, my heart filled with envy and with ache.

EDWARD. Charlotte, I have a confession to make.

CHARLOTTE. *(Aside, with a smile.)* He has a gift for getting my attention.

EDWARD. I must petition your heart about something.

CHARLOTTE. *(End aside.)* My heart will hear your case, but my mind shall judge it.

EDWARD. I wish to complicate our lives. *(Pause, avidly.)* For years our great dream was to come to the country and be *alone together*. I wanted to complete my travel journals, and have you copy them out in your own hand — so in that way, we could *travel in memory* to all the places that we were unable to travel together.

CHARLOTTE. Yes, and now that the park is finished —

EDWARD. I desire someone else. Someone new. *(Silence.)*

CHARLOTTE. I see. *(Pause.)* Well, please tell me. This "complication" of whom you speak —

EDWARD. It is the Captain. He is my oldest and dearest friend and he is being killed by *idleness*. He is a man of great talent and energy for whom the world (foolishly) professes no need. *I want him to live with us, Charlotte.* His expertise in matters of business, horticulture and design — all these things shall serve to improve our life here immeasurably. *(Edward stops, noticing Charlotte's wry smile.)* What is it?

CHARLOTTE. *That's* who you've been thinking of? *The Captain?*

EDWARD. Is that so strange?

CHARLOTTE. Well — no — but like any woman, I have an innate ability to recognize my rivals, so I imagined —

EDWARD. You imagined I'd been thinking of a *woman*?

CHARLOTTE. Is that so strange?

EDWARD. Yes. In fact, it is. *(Moving close to her.)* I lost you once, Charlotte, in my youth. But now, having regained you, I shall never lose you again. *(She stares at him, smiles a bit.)*

CHARLOTTE. I'm glad to hear that.

EDWARD. So, we are agreed. I will send for the Captain immediately.

CHARLOTTE. I have a premonition that no good will come of this. There is nothing more significant than the intervention of a third party. Many couples never recover from it.

EDWARD. But we are not like other people —

CHARLOTTE. I have made sacrifices, Edward — so that *nothing* would hinder our life here together. *(She touches his face, gently.)* I have no regrets. And no wish to change our plans. This has been the happiest summer of my life. *(They kiss, tenderly, then —)*

EDWARD. *(Aside, part frustration, part admiration.)* A woman, when arguing in this manner, is *invincible:* She is sensible — so you cannot contradict her. Affectionate — so you are glad to give in. Sensitive — so you do not want to hurt her. And finally, armed with *premonitions* — which leave you filled with *fear.*

CHARLOTTE. *(Moving away, with a smile.)* So, what now? Shall we call Mittler? This is the first real dispute of our marriage.

EDWARD. *(End aside.)* We have been lucky in that regard.

CHARLOTTE. Mittler is renowned for his ability to settle such issues. Shall we seek his help? *(Silence, then Edward goes to her, takes her hand.)*

EDWARD. No. I will write to the Captain. I will be friendly and sympathetic to his plight. But, I shall not extend my offer. And that will be that.

CHARLOTTE. Thank you. *(Charlotte removes a letter from her clothing and reads it, as —)*

EDWARD. *(Immediate aside, desperate.)* What have I done?! I am not accustomed to denying myself *anything.* For many years, the one thing I lacked in my life was Charlotte, my true love. But, in time, even that wish was granted. Her husband enlisted and was killed in battle, leaving her alone. Another man would have granted her a respectable period of mourning — but I pursued her *immediately* and showered her with an unseemly affection, until she, too, was mine. And my life was *complete.(Beat.)* Until today. Today I desire my dear friend, the Captain, at my side. For, if I had *that* — I assure you — I would want for *nothing else.*

CHARLOTTE. *(Folding the letter back up.)* I have changed my mind.

EDWARD. *(End aside.)* What's that?

CHARLOTTE. I agree to your plan. Invite the Captain to join us.

EDWARD. *(Delighted, confused.)* Charlotte —

CHARLOTTE. *(Kindly.)* Only remember this: where there is room for three, a *fourth* may follow. *(Music, under, as lights change, and the Captain enters, buoyantly.)*

THE CAPTAIN. I will do all I can to be *useful* to you, Edward. Your generous hospitality shall be a debt I repay in full. And Charlotte, if ever you should have need of me —

CHARLOTTE. Oh, I'm sure my husband will keep you quite busy. But, thank you.

EDWARD. I wanted you to see our new park — the jewel in our crown. I can take no credit for it, of course — it is Charlotte's doing, from beginning to end. *(Pause.)* Well, what do you think? *(As the Captain turns to the audience — the music stops, abruptly.)*

THE CAPTAIN. *(Aside.)* I am not easily pleased. Nature is no place for an amateur to try their hand. Charlotte — like all those who engage in a project for their own amusement — is clearly more concerned with having *something to do* than *doing what needs to be done.*

EDWARD. *(Brightly.)* Any comment would be appreciated.

THE CAPTAIN. *(Aside.)* This sort of person fumbles about with Nature — producing nothing but a hodge-podge that may grant a bit of common pleasure, but can *never fully satisfy.*

CHARLOTTE. Captain?

THE CAPTAIN. *(End aside, smiles.)* It's lovely.

EDWARD. I knew you'd be pleased.

CHARLOTTE. Thank you. *(An awkward silence — then, Charlotte to the rescue —)* Well, I must see about supper. I hope you won't mind, but I've planned a small celebration.

EDWARD. Charlotte, please, you know I —

CHARLOTTE. *(To the Captain.)* My husband deplores what he calls "festivities" — but today I have made an exception.

EDWARD. For what reason?

CHARLOTTE. I believe today is your nameday. Don't both of you have the given name of Otto? *(The Captain puts his arm around Edward.)*

THE CAPTAIN. *(With delight.)* Well, yes, in fact —

27

EDWARD. — That is what first brought us together as friends!

CHARLOTTE. Then a celebration is in order.

THE CAPTAIN. The "Two Ottos" — it always led to great confusion.

EDWARD. *(To Charlotte.)* So, I resigned the name to him — and I adopted the use of my middle name: "Edward."

CAPTAIN. *(To Charlotte.)* He knew that women preferred the name "Edward." It hung like honey on their lips.

EDWARD.   CHARLOTTE.

(With a laugh.) That is not why —   *(To Edward.)* Now, I see!

THE CAPTAIN. *(Playfully.)* And there I was, stuck with "Otto." It diminished my prospects considerably.

EDWARD. *(To Charlotte.)* What brought this to mind?

CHARLOTTE. *(To Edward.)* When we were married, you gave me the chalice from your boyhood. *(To the Captain.)* His parents had his initials inscribed upon it: an "O" and an "E" — intertwined.

EDWARD. We must show it to the Captain.

CHARLOTTE. First we must find it. It is somewhere on this estate in a trunk labeled: "Our Youth." *(As she goes.)* Enjoy the day, gentlemen. *(To the Captain.)* And welcome. *(Edward watches Charlotte disappear, as the Captain, once again, looks out at the vista.)*

EDWARD. Isn't she remarkable?

THE CAPTAIN. Indeed, she is.

EDWARD. *(Turning to the vista, proudly.)* And those poplars in the distance ... *majestic*, aren't they? *(The Captain nods.)* I planted them myself when I was a boy. They were just saplings then — but now they nearly dwarf the little stream beneath them. *(Stops, it dawns on him.)* You don't care for it, do you? *(The Captain stares at him, caught.)* You don't approve of how Charlotte's laid out the park. Confess it honestly.

THE CAPTAIN. The conception is not ... overly flawed.

EDWARD. *(Smiles.)* Otto, we've been friends for all our lives.

THE CAPTAIN. Yes, we have.

EDWARD. You know my darkest secrets and I am certain that I know yours.

THE CAPTAIN. Yes, you do.

EDWARD. So, please. The truth. *(The Captain looks at Edward, then out at the vista.)*

28

THE CAPTAIN. *(Definitively.)* I would flood it. I would flood it all.

EDWARD. I beg your pardon?

THE CAPTAIN. Not simply because Charlotte's work is naive and without merit — no, I would flood it because at one time what we see before us was, in fact, a large *lake*. And so it could be again. The stream could be dammed at the far end, and Nature would complete the rest. In a few months time, the water would fill the valley. A pier could be built, rowboats procured. And up here, overlooking it all, a pavilion — from where, on moonlit nights, the lake would shimmer in the darkness like a diamond. *(Edward looks at the Captain, then back at the vista.)*

EDWARD. How will we tell Charlotte?

THE CAPTAIN. We won't. Not at first. We shall busy ourselves with mapping the estate. And, if questioned, we will take our cue from the water which shall rise below us: we will enlighten her *incrementally. (Music under, as Edward gazes out at the vista once again. A reverie.)*

EDWARD. I see it. I see it all before me — as though it were not a plan, but something which had already come to pass.

THE CAPTAIN. You know, friend, your beloved poplars will not survive.

EDWARD. *(Simply, without regret.)* They are my youth. And my youth is gone. *(Music continues, as lights shift to —)*

A Drawing Room. Day.

The room requires only a table surrounded by a few chairs, a chaise lounge, and Edward's "reading chair." As the room is assembled — Charlotte enters, carrying the letter we saw her reading earlier. She is now in her full period costume. She is followed by Nicolas — the young schoolmaster.

CHARLOTTE. Thank you for coming in person. I've heard a great deal about you from my niece, Lucianne. She invokes your

29

name with a particular fondness: "Young Nicolas, the Schoolmaster" — you have made quite an impression.

NICOLAS. Your niece is the pride of our school. She has excelled at her studies in the same way, I'm sure, that she will excel in the world.

CHARLOTTE. All credit must go to my sister. It was she who raised Lucianne to such excellence — something I've never been called upon to do.

NICOLAS. You've no children of your own?

CHARLOTTE. No. *(She gestures for him to sit, which he does. Music has faded out.)* Your letter mentions a young woman at the school. An orphan in need of companionship.

NICOLAS. Yes.

CHARLOTTE. Having been raised an orphan myself, I feel great empathy for her. What's more, I have a strange affinity for her name: "Ottilie." It was a nickname of mine when I was a young girl.

NICOLAS. If I may, I would like to appeal to your heart.

CHARLOTTE. My heart is *awash* in such appeals. Just once, I would like to hear an appeal to my mind.

NICOLAS. During her years in school, Ottilie has had an anonymous benefactor. This person has made yearly contributions on her behalf — the amounts quite generous, indeed — but what she needs now is not financial help, but a *family*.

CHARLOTTE. *(Aside.)* And now a picture in my mind: Ottilie is a young girl. Upon seeing me, she throws her arms around my leg and holds on — with all her strength — as I stand above her, stroking her hair.

NICOLAS. If it were possible for her to be in your company, if you could visit her at school on a regular basis, staying a few days at a time —

CHARLOTTE. *(End aside.)* Young Nicolas, let me be clear: I have no intention of visiting your school.

NICOLAS. *(Confused.)* Why then did you summon me?

CHARLOTTE. This young woman, Ottilie — I want her to come live with us.

NICOLAS. I don't understand —

CHARLOTTE. She will have full run of the estate — our library, our music room, all the amenities of knowledge and pleasure which have been denied her. And further, and most to the point, I shall offer her not only my influence ... but my friendship.

NICOLAS. With due respect, I am not in the habit of encouraging my students to abandon their studies and retreat into the country.

CHARLOTTE. I trust you encourage them to *think*, do you not?

NICOLAS. Well, certainly —

CHARLOTTE. To place faith in the power of reason?

NICOLAS. Yes, of course, but —

CHARLOTTE. *Then let her decide.* Carry my offer to her and abide by her wishes. Will you do that? *(Silence. Standoff.)* You're fond of her, aren't you? You're fond of this young woman and now I'm about to steal her away.

NICOLAS. Why now?

CHARLOTTE. Pardon me?

NICOLAS. After all these years, why do you step forward now? *(Pause.)* Yes. I've read her records.

CHARLOTTE. Those records are confidential — they were sealed by order of —

NICOLAS. Yes, that's true and yes, I am fond of her — so I found a way to read them. They tell an interesting story.

CHARLOTTE. You mustn't tell my husband. He wouldn't approve that I've been her benefactor.

NICOLAS. And the adoption? *(Charlotte stares at him, then moves away.)* Ottilie's mother was your closest friend. And upon her death, you were instructed to adopt Ottilie as your daughter. The papers which make you her legal guardian are still there in her file. But, they were never signed. And Ottilie was sent away to an orphanage. *(Charlotte speaks quietly, choosing her words carefully.)*

CHARLOTTE. I have, of late, granted my husband his wish for camaraderie. But, the cost of my husband's joy, I'm afraid ... is my own loneliness. *(Pause.)* I require a confidant. I need Ottilie in the way she once needed me. *(Pause, desperately.)* Please — go to her. And offer her this life. I will abide by her decision.

NICOLAS. *(Stands, preparing to leave.)* It's a blessing you did not raise her. She's acquired none of your selfishness or deceit. She wishes only to provide for the contentment of others — and, in that way, is wiser than the world itself. *(Pause.)* I will keep your secret. I will say nothing to your husband. But, as for Ottilie, I should like permission to visit her.

CHARLOTTE. By all means. *(Pause.)* Thank you for your —

NICOLAS. Good day. *(Nicolas turns as goes, as — music plays, and a shaft of light rises on stage, revealing ... nothing. After a moment of silence — Mittler runs onstage and into the light. He stops, looking at the audience, catching his breath, then speaks —)*

MITTLER. I have, at best, a *complicated* occupation. I am a mediator. I resolve disputes that arise within the covenant of marriage. I am, therefore, a *very busy man.* My previous careers as a minister and a lawyer provide the cornerstone for my success, and rare is the couple who has not petitioned me for advice. I am vigilant. I am stubborn. And I am rigorously on guard against the greatest enemy of any marriage: *caprice.* I've only time enough to tell you two more things: I never enter a house unless there is a dispute to be solved. And, on my watch, not a single marriage has ended in divorce. *Not one.* (He stares at the audience, tips his hat, then ... runs off, as lights return to —)

The Drawing Room. Day.

Edward — now in his full period costume — and the Captain stand at the table. A large map is open on the table in front of them. A small case which holds the Captain's drafting and surveying equipment is nearby.

THE CAPTAIN. *(Referring to the map.)* Now: the lake I have proposed would stretch from the northern cliffs — here — to the — *(Music fades, as — Edward, seeing Charlotte entering, says —)*

EDWARD. You're right, Captain. Nothing stirs the memory like a map. It will be a great aid in reconstructing my travels. *(Charlotte remains at some distance from the table.)*

THE CAPTAIN. Good day, Charlotte.

CHARLOTTE. Have you begun work on your travel journals?

EDWARD. The Captain has proved himself indispensable.

CHARLOTTE. *(Lightly.)* I see I am easily replaced.

THE CAPTAIN.   EDWARD.
Oh, to the contrary —   Not at all —

CHARLOTTE. But, remember, Edward — when the journals are ready to be copied out, I still wish to do it in my own hand.

EDWARD. I would entrust them to no other. *(Charlotte now approaches the table.)*

CHARLOTTE. It is a splendid idea — to visualize your journeys in that way. *(She stops, seeing the map for what it is.)* This is our estate, is it not? *(The men are silent.)* Edward?

EDWARD. The Captain has agreed to survey the property. Isn't that generous of him? It has never been formally done — in all the years we've lived here.

CHARLOTTE. And to what purpose? *(Edward turns to the Captain for help.)*

THE CAPTAIN. If, for example, in time, you desire more ... *improvements* ... or *alterations* ...

CHARLOTTE. Do we, Edward?

EDWARD. Pardon?

CHARLOTTE. Do we desire more improvements?

EDWARD. *(Referring to the map.)* Well ... we've spoken of widening the road which leads into town. And the park, itself, may need ... a ... finishing touch or two.

CHARLOTTE. *(Looking at the map.)* A bench.

EDWARD. Pardon?

CHARLOTTE. It needs a bench. I've just this moment realized. It needs a bench — *(Taking a pencil and marking the map.)* — Right here. Near the cover of these trees. Don't you agree, Captain?

THE CAPTAIN. *(Noncommittal.)* A bench.

CHARLOTTE. Yes. And I shall see to that *myself.* *(Aside, as she rolls up the map.)* Men are such odd creatures. If I stood with a man at the edge of a lake, I can promise you what would happen: I would stare at the reflection of the trees in the water. And the man would pick up a stone and throw it into the lake. They see the world not as something to be affected by, but as something to *affect. (End aside, pleasantly.)* Here you are. *(Charlotte hands the*

33

map to the Captain, and starts off, saying —) Good day, gentlemen. *(Edward follows her, as the Captain moves away and retrieves his carrying case.)*

EDWARD. Charlotte, you should know that the Captain has only your best interests at heart.

CHARLOTTE. I'm glad to hear that.

EDWARD. Only today, in fact, he asked if his presence here had become burdensome. If, since his arrival, you hadn't grown lonely.

CHARLOTTE. And what did you say?

EDWARD. I didn't know. *(Pause, simply.)* I honestly didn't know. *(Music plays, as — Charlotte, then the Captain, and then Edward all turn and look upstage, seeing — Ottilie. She does not so much enter, as materialize. Her clothes are simple and ordinary ... but she is as lovely and poised as the music which is playing; her gaze as strong and pure as nature itself.)*

EDWARD. Charlotte ... who is this?

CHARLOTTE. I, too, wish to complicate our lives. *(Music continues, filling the theatre, as — Charlotte reaches out her arms to Ottilie. Ottilie is hesitant at first. She looks at Charlotte — then at Edward and the Captain — then back at Charlotte. Smiling now, Charlotte nods ... and Ottilie slowly approaches her. Both Edward and the Captain stare at Ottilie. Then each of them turn to the audience, and begin speaking at the same time —*)

EDWARD.	THE CAPTAIN.
(Aside.) For my part —	*(Aside.)* I am not —

(They each stop, realizing the other is speaking. The Captain gestures for Edward to go first. Edward demurs and insists the Captain speak first, which he does. Music continues, under.)

THE CAPTAIN. *(Aside.)* I am not immune to the allure of women. But, unlike men of my acquaintance, I seldom require more than a glance. I observe, take stock, and move on. I pride myself in the measured form of my response. *(His tone changes.)* But, never in my life had I seen a woman like this. She seemed the invention of some benevolent, over-achieving god. The force of her presence flooded the room and swept away all within it. She was, at once, as vital as nature ... as eternal as hope. *(The Captain exits, as Edward watches him go. Charlotte continues to stroke Ottilie's hair.)*

34

EDWARD. *(Aside, flatly.)* For my part, I hoped that — *whoever she was* — she'd keep Charlotte busy while the Captain and I went about our work. *(Edward exits, as, suddenly — Ottilie falls to the ground, grasping Charlotte by the legs, holding her tightly, desperately. Charlotte is flummoxed for a moment ... then begins to softly stroke Ottilie's hair. Music fades. Ottilie lifts her face to Charlotte. She beams with affection.)*

CHARLOTTE. Oh, Ottilie — why this show of humility?

OTTILIE. I remember when I was a young girl and reached no higher than your knee. Even then, I was certain of your love. *(Charlotte touches Ottilie's face.)*

CHARLOTTE. That love has brought you here, and shall sustain you. *(Charlotte helps Ottilie to her feet.)* Nothing more need be said.

OTTILIE. But the men, will I be disturbing their —

CHARLOTTE. Beauty is everywhere a welcome guest. Did the coachman carry in your things?

OTTILIE. I've nothing to bring.

CHARLOTTE. But your clothes, your belongings —

OTTILIE. There's nothing. Only myself.

CHARLOTTE. My dear girl ... *(Stares at her, with empathy.)* You have your mother's eyes.

OTTILIE. Will you tell me about her? I was only eight years old ... *(Her voice trails off.)*

CHARLOTTE. Of course I will. *(More brightly.)* But first I will show you to your room.

OTTILIE. Madame, if you don't mind —

CHARLOTTE. I am Charlotte to you now. Though your mother used to call me Ottilie.

OTTILIE. I was named after you, then?

CHARLOTTE. *(Quietly.)* I suppose you were.

OTTILIE. May I meet the servants and be shown the workings of the house?

CHARLOTTE. Whatever for?

OTTILIE. I owe you a great debt. My life at school was unbearable, but now you have freed me from that place.

CHARLOTTE. But, Ottilie, I didn't bring you here to work.

OTTILIE. I wish to be of use to you. When my mother died, I prayed they would send me to live with you. At the orphanage, I pleaded with them, crying myself to sleep. But now, all these years later, my prayers have been answered. *(Music under, as a shaft of light isolates —)*

A Hallway. Day.

Lucianne is holding a letter. She looks around. Then, she carefully opens the letter and begins reading it, as — Nicolas passes, walking behind her.

NICOLAS. Lucianne, it's time for class. The other girls are waiting.
LUCIANNE. Your penmanship changes, did you know that? When you make notations on our papers in class, your writing is bold and simple and to the point. *(Nicolas has stopped. Lucianne holds up the letter. Music fades.)* But when you write a love letter, your pen is lighter, your letters dressed in flourishes, filled with little sweeps and serifs — *commes les oiseaux qui s'envolent.*
NICOLAS. Where did you get that?
LUCIANNE. I have been *too good.* Here I am, nearly finished with my schooling, and I know nothing about *mischief.* So, I am teaching myself.
NICOLAS. You went through my desk. *(Growing angry.)* Lucianne, what possessed you to —
LUCIANNE. What's delicious is that the first page is missing … so I'm not sure for whom these words are intended. *(Turns to him, hopeful, seductive.)* Ils sont pour moi?
NICOLAS. Lucianne —
LUCIANNE. *(Reading from the letter.)* "My life, at present, offers nothing but the chance to participate in the boredom of others. You alone are my solace; my escape. When I think of your eyes, and your chin, and your tiny, ivory hands … I am rendered helpless. I cannot read, nor speak. And I've no need for sleep, since thinking of you has made dreaming unnecessary." *(She approaches him, stands very close to him —)* Young Nicolas the schoolmas-

ter ... you are a man after all. *(She runs the edge of the letter slowly, gently down the side of his face — a caress.)* Teach me. Teach me the mischief of men. *(Staying close to her, he gently takes the letter from her hand. She looks in his eyes for a moment, then — she touches him playfully on the nose, and — runs off, giggling and laughing with joy, as — music plays, and lights shift back to —)*

The Drawing Room. Evening.

Charlotte sits on the chaise, wearing eyeglasses, making notes in a large ledger. Edward sits in "his" chair, reading a book. It is, of course, the book from the prologue. The Captain sits at the table, assembling a rather impressive scale model of the estate.

Ottilie, wearing an apron, carries a small tray with three cups of tea. [Goethe: She walks so lightly that none can hear her footsteps.] Ottilie serves first the Captain — who smiles, warmly; then Edward — who merely nods, not meeting her eye; then she brings the third cup to Charlotte. She stands before Charlotte for a long moment. Finally —

OTTILIE. *(Softly.)* Charlotte. *(Music stops.)*
CHARLOTTE. *(Startled.)* Ottilie — how long have you been standing there?
OTTILIE. Only a moment.
CHARLOTTE. I didn't even hear you walk in.
THE CAPTAIN. She treads as lightly as an angel.
OTTILIE. Here is your tea.
CHARLOTTE. Thank you — but I think not tonight. *(Ottilie turns to leave, with the tea.)* Why don't you have it? *(Ottilie stops.)* Yes. Why don't you take off your apron and join us? I insist.
OTTILIE. I've still work I wish to do.
CHARLOTTE. You work night and day without a break. It's

worrisome to me. *(Gestures to a chair at the table.)* So, please. *(Ottilie looks at Edward — who does not look up from his book. She then looks at the Captain — who pulls back the chair, saying —)*

THE CAPTAIN. It would be our pleasure. *(Ottilie looks once again at Charlotte — who nods. Ottilie removes her apron and sits at the table, the third cup of tea in front of her. The Captain lifts his tea … and Ottilie follows suit. They each sip their tea, as — Charlotte closes her ledger and removes her glasses.)*

CHARLOTTE. You have been of great help to us, Ottilie.

OTTILIE. I've tried only to model myself after you.

THE CAPTAIN. Charlotte is a master of organization.

OTTILIE. I shall hope to learn that from her. And from you, Captain? What shall I hope to learn from you?

CHARLOTTE. *(Coyly.)* The Captain is a master of the surprise attack. One never knows which part of the estate he shall set his sights on next. It is his military training, no doubt.

OTTILIE. Is that true?

THE CAPTAIN. I have known the rigors of battle, but such days are behind me. My efforts now are directed not at vanquishing my foes, but in securing for my friends — Edward and Charlotte — *their long-sought tranquillity.*

OTTILIE. *(Deeply affected by this sentiment.)* That is a lovely thought.

CHARLOTTE. Yes, it is.

THE CAPTAIN. And from you, Edward?

EDWARD. *(Not looking up from his book.)* Hmm?

THE CAPTAIN. What shall Ottilie hope to learn from the master of the house?

EDWARD. *(Holding up his book.)* She will learn that we are ruled not by reason, but by *science* — by the chemical impulses which fire and flare within us.

THE CAPTAIN. *(A favorite topic.)* Indeed!

CHARLOTTE. *(A smile, to Ottilie.)* I'm afraid a lecture is coming. *(Edward and Charlotte listen with enthusiasm, as — During the following, the Captain demonstrates his point — using Ottilie, from time to time, to help him. The Captain uses his teacup and saucer to represent the two elements he refers to.)*

THE CAPTAIN. Nature itself is built on the affinity which two elements have for one another. And when these two unite — marrying their distinct qualities together — a new and powerful substance is born.

CHARLOTTE. And it is indissoluble. *(The Captain now uses Ottilie's teacup to represent the third element —)*

THE CAPTAIN. Unless a *third* element is introduced.

OTTILIE. What happens then?

THE CAPTAIN. The unified state is dissolved.

CHARLOTTE. Permanently?

THE CAPTAIN. Until such time as the third element is *removed* — allowing the original elements to reunite.

CHARLOTTE. *(With a smile.)* As well they should.

EDWARD. But rather than removing the disruptive third element, couldn't the scientist, instead, introduce a *fourth*? *(The Captain now uses Ottilie's saucer to represent the fourth element —)*

THE CAPTAIN. *(With great enthusiasm.)* Yes, indeed! These cases are the most noteworthy of all —

OTTILIE. Why is that?

THE CAPTAIN. Where four elements — previously joined together in two pairs — are brought into contact —

EDWARD. Causing them to abandon their *previous unions* —

THE CAPTAIN. And join together in *newly formed pairs. (The Captain and Ottilie switch the teacups accordingly —)*

CHARLOTTE. Which proves that beyond that which we *desire* —

EDWARD. — Awaits that which we are *destined for. (Music plays, as — This thought settles, with pleasure, upon each of them, as — Charlotte turns to the audience, saying —)*

CHARLOTTE. *(Aside.)* It's remarkable to look back upon that time. The four of us together — with no bitterness, no confusion between us. It seems impossible, but there actually was a time when all of us, without exception, were *happy. (Music continues, as — Charlotte dons her glasses and reopens her ledger. Edward has returned to his chair, reading. Ottilie sips her tea and watches the Captain work on the model of the estate.)*

THE CAPTAIN. *(Aside.)* My good friend at my side. A lovely young woman to light my days. And the steady hand of Charlotte … steering me through these, the best and final years of my life.

OTTILIE. *(Aside.)* I vowed that night to remember the Captain's words: to do nothing that would disrupt the tranquillity of this house.

EDWARD. *(Aside, looking up from his book.)* I have never been more at peace. As I told you, I lacked only the presence of my dear friend at my side. Now, I require *nothing more. (Edward returns to his book. As Charlotte speaks, she moves behind the chair in which Edward is reading — looking down at the book in his hands.)*

CHARLOTTE. *(Aside.)* This state of grace held for several weeks. Then, in imitation, perhaps, of our own hearts, it began to give way ... *(Music out, as — The sounds of a distant storm are heard.)*

EDWARD. Charlotte.

CHARLOTTE. *(End aside, reading over his shoulder.)* Yes?

EDWARD. There is something I've asked you never to do.

CHARLOTTE. *(Having no idea.)* And what is that? *(Edward closes the book with force.)*

EDWARD. There is no greater affront to one's personal pleasure than to have someone *read over their shoulder. (Thrusts the book towards her.)* Here! Take it! It's of no use to me now.

CHARLOTTE. *(Not taking the book.)* Edward, I'm sorry —

EDWARD. *(Moving away.)* How often must I tell you?! Perhaps you consider this an outlandish request, but if so, why have the Captain and Ottilie — in all their weeks here — seen fit to avoid such an egregious display of disregard?! *(Quick aside.)* Before you judge me, please hear me out. *(End aside.)* One reads a book to have a *private conversation.* It is a harmless, sweet diversion from one's life. And, what's more, it is emblematic of one's fundamental need — even in the most harmonious marriage — for a true moment of solitude. When you deny me that, when you come between me and own imaginings, I feel as though I am being *torn in half. (He tosses the book offstage, then states, simply:)* I shall never open that book again. *(They are all motionless for a long moment. Ottilie and the Captain are staring at Charlotte. Edward, too, ultimately turns and looks at her. Thunder and rain are heard as the storm approaches.)*

CHARLOTTE. *(Aside.)* Edward has always praised my ability to deflect the "difficult moment." I have a gift for steering a room away from acrimony and back toward calm. Look at them — they've grown to expect it of me. And on this day — once again —

I did not disappoint. I ignored Edward's outburst and gracefully changed the subject. However, it was the last time I ever did so. *(End aside, to the Captain.)* I see your scale model is nearly complete.

THE CAPTAIN. *(Pause.)* Well ... yes. Yes, it is.

CHARLOTTE. *(Going to the model.)* But, I've noticed it's missing my park bench. I shall be installing it tomorrow. *(Turns to Ottilie.)* Would you bring me some tea, dear?

OTTILIE. Yes, of course. *(Ottilie leaves, taking her apron with her, as — Charlotte lifts some small object — which can depict "the bench" — and places it on the model.)*

CHARLOTTE. There. That will do. Merely an oversight, I'm sure. Now, I wonder if you could fill me in on your plans. For example, what is this structure you've been toying with?

EDWARD. The Captain has had the splendid idea to locate a pavilion atop the hillside. In that way —

CHARLOTTE. In that way, one will have a lovely view of my park. *(To the Captain, happily.)* What a wonderful idea! May I help you with its placement?

EDWARD. Actually, Charlotte — since this is the Captain's area of expertise —

THE CAPTAIN. No, Edward, I think it's only fitting that Charlotte be allowed to place the pavilion. *(Gestures to the scale model.)* Please. *(Charlotte sits at the table and adjusts the placement of the pavilion during the following. The Captain stands behind her. A persistent rain is now falling.)*

CHARLOTTE. Well, to have a clear view of the gardens I have planted below, it would need to be very close to this edge ... here ... *(Ottilie enters with a cup of tea, which she sets near Charlotte.)* And, perhaps, angled a bit to the east to catch the morning sun. *(Pleased.)* What do you think? *(The Captain nods and looks at Edward. Edward does not respond.)* Edward?

EDWARD. I had a different idea. Or, to be fair, Ottilie did. *(Charlotte looks to Ottilie, as — Edward adjusts the pavilion accordingly.)* She mentioned that moving the pavilion away from the edge would be safer for any children who played there.

CHARLOTTE. That is a valid concern, but —

EDWARD. Beyond that, it was her idea to orient the pavilion towards the west — this would take advantage of the sunset —

CHARLOTTE. Indeed, but I think —

EDWARD. *(With passion.)* And, what's more, it would fully remove the main buildings of the estate from one's view ... so that one felt, upon entering the pavilion, that he had left the rest of the world behind. *(Charlotte looks to Ottilie.)*

CHARLOTTE. You consulted her on all these things?

THE CAPTAIN. Not formally, no. They simply came up in conversation.

OTTILIE. And they weren't my ideas, at all.

EDWARD. Of course they were.

OTTILIE. *(To Edward.)* No, they were yours. From your travel journals. You describe a hillside in Italy which is laid out in the same manner. *(Silence.)*

CHARLOTTE. *(To Edward.)* You gave her your journals to read?

EDWARD. *(The truth.)* No, I didn't.

OTTILIE. I was putting the rooms in order. And in Edward's study, I saw the journals, stacked away in a corner. I determined to shelve them in chronological order. And that led me to read from them.

CHARLOTTE. *(Sharp.)* Those journals are private. They are a record of Edward's life which he intends to share only with me.

OTTILIE. *(Quietly.)* I understand.

CHARLOTTE. Good.

OTTILIE. *(Simply.)* You may dismiss me now and send me away. It is the punishment I deserve. *(Charlotte looks at Ottilie — then to Edward, who says nothing. Then, Charlotte approaches Ottilie, lifts her bowed head, looks in her eyes.)*

CHARLOTTE. *(With full forgiveness.)* I will never dismiss you. This is your home.

EDWARD. *(Aside, on edge.)* And there in my mind, this picture: Ottilie's hands, turning the pages of my journals. *Nothing* provokes me to anger like having my books read, my private papers rifled through. *(Pause, he looks at Ottilie, his tone softens.)* And, yet ...

THE CAPTAIN. Perhaps we should walk up there and have a look.

CHARLOTTE. Walk up where?

THE CAPTAIN. To the hillside.

CHARLOTTE. At this hour?

THE CAPTAIN. Ottilie? Would you care to join me?

CHARLOTTE. But it's pouring rain —

THE CAPTAIN. *(In reference to the model.)* Our mistake is that we have been looking at things in miniature. It's time to have our eyes opened to the full measure of the situation.

CHARLOTTE. But you'll —

THE CAPTAIN. *(Looking at Charlotte, with a smile.)* So let's disobey Charlotte and run up there in the rain. What do you say? *(Ottilie nods and exits. The Captain follows. Edward busies himself with the model.)*

CHARLOTTE. May I ask you something?

EDWARD. Of course.

CHARLOTTE. What do you think of her?

EDWARD. Of Ottilie? *(Charlotte nods.)* I have no opinion of her.

CHARLOTTE. After all these months, no opinion at all?

EDWARD. None.

CHARLOTTE. That's quite a trick, Edward — to maintain an ongoing absence of opinion.

EDWARD. *(Hoping to put an end to this.)* She is pleasant and amusing and extremely hard-working. She seems to anticipate our every need and, in doing so, has made herself indispensable to us. Does that suffice?

CHARLOTTE. And her beauty?

EDWARD. What of it?

CHARLOTTE. She is a feast for the eyes. How can you fail to mention that?

EDWARD. *(Aside.)* As you know, it is impossible for a man to emerge unscathed from this line of questioning.

CHARLOTTE. I have watched you and the Captain cut short your work in order to sit and converse in her presence. *Not to speak to her*, mind you — but simply to place your life in proximity to hers.

EDWARD. *(End aside.)* She is a very good listener. And her beauty — like any unexpected gift of Nature — is a welcome addition to our home. What is the meaning of this? You seem determined to test me on this point.

CHARLOTTE. *(Aside.)* And of course I was. And it was not the first time. *(As Charlotte speaks, music plays, and — a shaft of moonlight reveals an upper window — identical to the beginning of the play. Framed in the window is Ottilie's unclothed back.)* One evening, I had gone to Ottilie's room and given her a beautiful gown of mine. As she stood there, preparing to try it on, I looked over her shoulder and out the window. There in the courtyard below was Edward, gazing up at us. I began to close the shutters — but then stopped. I wanted Edward to look at her. I wanted him to see her this way — the moonlight washing over her back like a caress. *(The image — and the music — begins to fade away.)* The next morning I studied him for any sign of interest in her ... and found none. *(End aside.)* I worry about the Captain.

EDWARD. In what way?

CHARLOTTE. The Captain has reached the age when men are finally capable of love. And with Ottilie so near, and so blessed with a young woman's charms —

EDWARD. The Captain is a man of the world and will — I'm sure — modulate his behavior to suit the situation. *(The rain gradually subsides. Edward moves to his chair and sits — without his book.)*

CHARLOTTE. Even so, while he's here I think Ottilie and I should sleep in the east wing — and you and the Captain in the west. Also, as a precaution, I shall endeavor to spend more time with the Captain. I shall make myself necessary to his work on the pavilion, and — *(Immediate aside.)* — I am having a thought as I am talking and that thought is this: I am determined to come between the Captain and Ottilie. But for what reason?

EDWARD. And?

CHARLOTTE. *(End aside.)* And I may even solicit his advice on improving the park. Do you think the Captain would welcome that?

EDWARD. I know he has strong feelings about the park.

CHARLOTTE. Splendid.

EDWARD. And what of Ottilie?

CHARLOTTE. I place her in your capable hands. *(Pause.)* Look ... the storm has passed. *(Ottilie enters, going directly to Charlotte.)* Ottilie? I thought you were going to accompany the Captain.

OTTILIE. May I speak with you?

CHARLOTTE. Certainly. Both Edward and I will gladly listen. *(Ottilie looks, pointedly, in the direction of Edward.)*

OTTILIE. I'm sorry, but I'd hoped to —

CHARLOTTE. There are no secrets in this house, Ottilie. You may speak to us both. I insist. *(With some reluctance, Ottilie steps into their midst.)*

OTTILIE. *(Quietly.)* Teach me to love. Some force has laid siege to my heart. Never have I felt such rapture, such chaos within me. So, please, teach me what to make of these feelings.

CHARLOTTE. You must celebrate them. There will be no love like your first.

OTTILIE. But, I'm afraid it's wrong. That I will cause suffering where I least intend it.

CHARLOTTE. It is an older man, isn't it? Someone in this house? I was just now telling Edward of my suspicions. *(Ottilie seems close to tears. Charlotte holds her.)* My dear girl, you've done nothing wrong. Your love is true and pure. And no matter the result, you must cherish this feeling — for never again will love be so new. *(Charlotte and Ottilie exit, arm in arm, as — lights isolate Edward, in his chair.)*

EDWARD. *(Aside.)* At the time of Ottilie's arrival, my life was, once again, complete. But she has made it a point to learn my habits and opinions, my likes and dislikes in all things — large or small — and to anticipate, with accuracy, my every desire ... *(Ottilie has reappeared, holding Edward's book. She walks to his chair ... puts the book into his hands ... and leaves, as he continues to speak —)* In doing so, she has endeared herself to my heart. Very quietly — and to my great surprise — she has produced in me a need that only she can fulfill. *(Pause.)* What causes the heart to enlarge in this way? And to what end? *(Music, as lights shift to —)*

The Hillside. Sunset.

Charlotte and the Captain enter and look out at the vista. Charlotte is pointing to something far in the distance —

CHARLOTTE. Do you see it? Beyond that grove of trees, near the tall fountain — do you see it?

THE CAPTAIN. No, I don't quite ... *(She leans in very close to him and shows him where she is pointing —)*

CHARLOTTE. Further to this side — and up a bit — *there.*

45

THE CAPTAIN. Yes — I see it — but it's only a dot from here.

CHARLOTTE. It is a *very fine bench*. Soon, I shall take you there and show you in person. I would like your opinion on where I had it placed. May I ask that of you? *(The Captain is silent, as — the music fades out.)* Captain?

THE CAPTAIN. It has been a pleasure to be in your company of late.

CHARLOTTE. The pleasure has been mine.

THE CAPTAIN. But I fear that our comfort together has enabled me to prolong a deception — a deception which I myself put in place. I shall not appeal to your heart, for I am not worthy of that. But, let me please appeal to your mind.

CHARLOTTE. *(A smile.)* I welcome such an appeal. *(The Captain looks at Charlotte, then out at the vista before them.)*

THE CAPTAIN. I want you to imagine never picking a flower from your garden. Never walking the pathways through your park; never wading in its stream. I want you to imagine, in fact, the destruction of all you've envisioned, all you've worked for, all that you've held as a source of beauty deep within your heart. And I want you to know that I alone shall be the cause of that destruction. *(He turns to her, taking her arms in his hands.)* I need your help, Charlotte. I am about to do something dreadful, something which only you — and your strong sense of purpose — can forestall.

CHARLOTTE. *(Backing away.)* Before you say more, I must confess something. I'm aware of what you're going to tell me, and I —

THE CAPTAIN. So you've *known*?

CHARLOTTE. Yes.

THE CAPTAIN. For *how long*?

CHARLOTTE. I saw it in your notes a few days ago — quite by accident, I assure you —

THE CAPTAIN. *(Confused.)* In my *notes?*

CHARLOTTE. Yes.

THE CAPTAIN. But I've told no one! And I've certainly not put it in writing for all to see! But let me now confess it:

CHARLOTTE. *You are flooding this valley.*

THE CAPTAIN. *(Nearly overlapping.)* I am falling in love. (Silence. It's out.)

CHARLOTTE. Pardon me?

THE CAPTAIN. A man spends his life awaiting the "substantial event" — the experience which shall define him. And, before I arrived here, I was convinced that my character had been forged on the battlefield; that those years of combat were the substantial event of my life. But I was mistaken, wasn't I?

CHARLOTTE. *(Pause.)* Yes. And you are not alone.

THE CAPTAIN. *(Amazed.)* I'm not?

CHARLOTTE. No. Ottilie has told me of her feelings. For my part, though, I do not fully approve of you falling in love with her.

THE CAPTAIN. *You. (Pause, simply.)* I am falling in love with you. *(Silence.)*

CHARLOTTE. *(Very quietly.)* I have forgotten how to have this conversation. All reason has raced from my mind.

THE CAPTAIN. Charlotte, it has been like a fever. And I thought that saying it out loud — confessing it to you directly — would break its hold on me. But, having said it once, I wish only to say it again and again.

CHARLOTTE. You and I are serious-minded people, known for our steady behavior and self control. Don't you see? — it is in the hearts of people like us that this sort of affection is most dangerous. *(She now walks up very close to him, putting her face very close to his. We think she may be about to kiss him ... but, instead, she turns and looks out at the vista.)* I shall miss the paths I used to walk on. *(Music, as lights shift to —)*

The Drawing Room. Dusk.

Edward stands at the table, looking at the scale model. Ottilie enters with a lit candelabra, which she proceeds to place on the table. As she does so ... Edward notices the locket which dangles from Ottilie's neck.

EDWARD. Careful. *(Ottilie stops.)* Your locket. I was afraid it would touch the flame.

OTTILIE. How clumsy of me.

EDWARD. It's very beautiful.

OTTILIE. Thank you. I'm sorry to disturb your work. I shall —

EDWARD. Whose picture is inside? If I may ask.

OTTILIE. *(Opening the locket.)* It's empty. I hoped one day to locate my father. And to ask him — in place of his love — for a picture. But my mother and I never found him.

EDWARD. I'm sorry. *(Edward returns to the scale model, and — Ottilie continues to stare at him.)*

OTTILIE. *(With no other motive.)* May I ask something of you?

EDWARD. Certainly.

OTTILIE. Will you unfasten it for me? *(He looks at her. Then, stands and walks behind her. She gracefully lifts her hair, revealing her neck.)* Do you see the clasp?

EDWARD. Yes. *(Edward, as calmly as possible, unfastens the clasp … and the locket is released into Ottilie's hands.)* There you are. *(Music fades away, as — Edward looks into her eyes.)* It's so lovely. Why would you —

OTTILIE. I needn't wear it. Now that I am here, in this house, I am no longer in search of love.

EDWARD. *(Aside.)* And a stone fell from my heart.

OTTILIE. I'm very sorry about your journals. I had no right to look through them.

EDWARD. *(End aside.)* No, you didn't. But, you do now. *(She looks at him.)* You have my permission to read them.

OTTILIE. *(Quietly.)* I couldn't do that. Charlotte told me they were —

EDWARD. I have seen your drawings. On various papers to be discarded, I've seen the sketches you've made.

OTTILIE. You were not meant to see those.

EDWARD. Then we each have violated the other. *(Pause.)* Often as I traveled, I wished for the ability to draw. A moonless night in Venice; the fireworks exploding over the canals. Oh, how I ached to record such things with pictures … and not with the cold machinery of words.

OTTILIE. I've never seen fireworks.

EDWARD. Perhaps one day you will. And perhaps you'll draw them for me, inside the pages of my journals. *(Aside.)* And she said nothing. She stood there, looking at me. And I prayed this moment would hold forever.

OTTILIE. *(Soft, but firm.)* I'm sorry. But, it would be wrong. *(He looks at her for a long moment.)*

EDWARD. *(End aside.)* Of course you're right.

OTTILIE. Charlotte is waiting. Excuse me.

EDWARD. There's a letter for you here. *(Lifting it, looking at it.)* I believe it's from Nicolas, the young schoolmaster. I've come to recognize his writing. The "O" which begins your name is drawn with such grandeur — it must have taken him the better part of a week.

OTTILIE. He is very kind to me. *(Edward hands Ottilie the letter, saying —)*

EDWARD. And very fortunate. To be a young man whose affections are unencumbered. *(Ottilie looks at Edward ... nods ... then leaves. Aside.)* I had gone, for a moment, to the very edge of my life. But once she left the room, God be thanked, my sanity returned — and the calm comfort of my home embraced me once again. *(Pause, more quietly.)* Until I thought of her hands. The way they moved when she did the simplest of things. It was into those hands that I — like her locket before me — was about to fall. And I told no one. Not even her. Because this was a dream ... and a dream needs no accomplice. *(A phrase of music, as lights shift quickly to —)*

An Entryway. Night.

A small area of light will suffice. Mittler approaches Charlotte — who is wearing a long, beautiful robe.

CHARLOTTE. What are you doing here at this hour?

MITTLER. Whosoever would attack the state of marriage — they must reckon with me! I am a very busy man, so speak to me with purpose: what is the nature of the dispute?

CHARLOTTE. I have no idea what you're —

MITTLER. I was riding into town and my horse suddenly turned down the lane and galloped for your house. I can assure you that does not happen without cause.

CHARLOTTE. And I can assure you that there's no dispute to be solved here.

MITTLER. Who's in this house right now?

CHARLOTTE. Edward and myself.

MITTLER. And who else?

CHARLOTTE. Our dear friends — Ottilie and the Captain.

MITTLER. And is another friend here?

CHARLOTTE. Who are you —

MITTLER. A friend of the idle and impatient. A friend named "Caprice" — is he here?

CHARLOTTE. I don't know what you're —

MITTLER. For if you welcome him into your home — *be on guard*. He shall quickly have full run of your life.

CHARLOTTE. *(Firmly.)* Mr. Mittler, I will ask you to leave. You are not needed here.

MITTLER. For your sake, I hope that's true. *(Mittler rushes off, and — music plays, as Charlotte turns and enters —)*

The Drawing Room. Night.

Edward sits in his chair, reading the book we saw him toss away earlier. His jacket is now off. Sitting on the arm of the chair is Ottilie. She is reading the book over Edward's shoulder. Each is relaxed, content. Charlotte stops when she sees them. She watches them read the book together. Edward and Ottilie are never aware of Charlotte's presence. After a moment, a shaft of light isolates — Charlotte, alone.

CHARLOTTE. *(Aside.)* Later that night, I heard footsteps in the hallway. I sat up in bed, my heart racing — for I knew who was out there: *it was the Captain.* In an act of brazen, unbidden courage he had come to me. *(A shaft of light — opposite Charlotte — reveals — Edward, alone. They do not turn to each other until noted.)*

EDWARD. *(Aside.)* I ran outside and roamed the grounds of the estate for hours — my mind enraptured with the secret I now possessed. Finally, I could wait no longer.

CHARLOTTE. And then — in answer to my most avid prayers — there were footsteps just outside my room —

EDWARD. I entered the estate and went to her room — possessed by a boldness I had never known —

CHARLOTTE. And then —

EDWARD. Very softly, I knocked on Ottilie's door —

CHARLOTTE. My voice cried out "Who is it?" — and my heart gave way to tears —

EDWARD. As I stood at Ottilie's door, I heard crying. It was coming from Charlotte's room.

CHARLOTTE. I prayed he would answer me —

EDWARD. I was trapped —

CHARLOTTE. Again I cried out "Who is there?" —

EDWARD. I heard Charlotte's voice and knew she was awake —

CHARLOTTE. But in my heart I *knew* —

EDWARD. I knew she'd heard me in the hall —

CHARLOTTE. I *knew* it was the Captain —

EDWARD. So, I knocked on *her* door — on *Charlotte's* door — *(Music builds, as — Edward and Charlotte now walk into and share an area of light, facing each other, their voices filled with a reckless and relentless passion —)*

CHARLOTTE. And I left my bed and raced across the room —

EDWARD. And the door opened —

CHARLOTTE. And there stood the Captain! *(Far upstage, the Captain appears in a shaft of light, looking at Charlotte, as — she gently touches Edward's face with her fingers.)* And from the lips of the Captain, came a voice … it was *Edward's voice* —

EDWARD. *(End aside, to Charlotte.)* I was downstairs and I heard you crying.

CHARLOTTE. *(As she touches his face.)* And at that moment, *I told myself everything a woman can tell herself.* That this madness would pass; that time alone can heal such torments. But, looking through my tears at Edward, *I still could see the Captain standing before me.* His spirit hovered there — filling my room and haunting my bed.

EDWARD. And so I made a vow. That I would visit your room and comfort you.

CHARLOTTE. *(End aside, to Edward.)* I knew you would. I knew you'd come for me.

EDWARD. *(Aside, looking at Charlotte.)* And on this night, *imagination asserted its rights over reality.*

CHARLOTTE. Stay with me.

EDWARD. As I stood before my wife, *I was looking into the eyes of Ottilie. (Opposite the Captain, Ottilie appears in a shaft of light — looking at Edward.)*

CHARLOTTE. Tonight alone I will be yours.

EDWARD. *(Doing so.)* And I took her in my arms —

CHARLOTTE. *(Aside, facing Edward, holding him.)* And I closed my eyes —

EDWARD. And there in the heat of this blissful seduction —

CHARLOTTE. Something of a miracle occurred —

EDWARD. *The absent and the present were intertwined —*

CHARLOTTE. *My imagination granted me what my life could not —*

EDWARD. *And the darkness of night held our secret. (Crescendo of music, as — Edward and Charlotte kiss, passionately, and — the light on them grows achingly bright, as — the images of Ottilie and the Captain fade away — And with a final flourish of music, the lights rush to black.)*

ACT TWO

Music under, as a shaft of light reveals — Ottilie. She speaks to the audience.

OTTILIE. Where I am standing a wall will be built. The rock wall which will dam the stream and hold back the force of the newly made lake. When I ask Edward how something can be made to withstand such pressure, he merely smiles, as if to say, "It is my secret." *(Pause.)* "I think about him. I contrive ways to see him. And when he is away, my imagination grants me that which my life cannot." *(Pause.)* These are words from a book which Edward gave me. Words he had taken care to underline — for remembrance. As for me, I underlined a separate passage: *(From memory.)* "With each passing day, I hear something in the distance. It is a storm, gathering force, at the far edge of my life. How shall I forestall it? And if it arrives, how shall I hold back the power of its wrath?" *(Lights expand to reveal —)*

The Hillside. Late Afternoon. Weeks Later.

The area has been prepared for a celebration. A wooden platform is in place, decorated with wildflowers and ribbons. Immediately in front of the platform is a brightly colored piece of fabric which fully covers a large, rectangular stone.

A man's hat flies on and lands at center. It is quickly followed by Lucianne — who rushes on, buoyantly. She is being chased — and not with pleasure — by Nicolas. Ottilie turns and watches — unseen by Lucianne and Nicolas, as — music continues, under.

LUCIANNE. It's here! Your hat is here! *(She picks up the hat, as — Nicolas lunges for it, falling to the ground, empty-handed.)*
NICOLAS. Lucianne, I am not in the mood for this game of yours —
LUCIANNE. Young Nicolas the schoolmaster — you are *too studious.*
NICOLAS. Give me my — *(He grabs for the hat, but she puts it behind her back and moves away, quickly.)*
LUCIANNE. You must learn how to play — and I will be your teacher! *(As she prepares to fling the hat offstage — Nicolas grabs her from behind, stopping her.)*
NICOLAS. Stop it! *(She enjoys his embrace, and does not release the hat. Speaks, seductively …)*
LUCIANNE. *Vous apprenez tres rapidement.*
NICOLAS. *(Arms around her, still trying to grab the hat.)* Lucianne — *(Lucianne now sees Ottilie. She keeps a tight hold on Nicolas while saying to Ottilie —)*
LUCIANNE. Oh, Ottilie — he's like all the rest — he must always have his hands on me.
NICOLAS. *(Upon seeing Ottilie.)* No — please — you don't underst — *(Lucianne "breaks away" from Nicolas.)*
LUCIANNE. As to your proposal, I shall need time to consider it. You are not the first to approach me … though you do have the softest lips. *(To Ottilie.)* If only young Nicolas could teach as well as he kisses.
NICOLAS. Lucianne, that's enough —
LUCIANNE. *(Tossing the hat to him, finally.)* Au revoir, mon amour! *(Lucianne rushes off, with a laugh, as — Nicolas and Ottilie look at one another.)*
NICOLAS. She imagines it all. I've made her no proposal. And, as for kissing, she is not the woman I desire. *(Silence.)* I so hoped to hear from you, Ottilie. All the letters I've sent … and nothing in return. Your silence, what does it mean?
OTTILIE. My heart is full.

54

NICOLAS. I see.

OTTILIE. Filled to bursting with feelings I've never known.

NICOLAS. *(Hopeful.)* And mine as well. How lucky for this day — that we are together and can now share these — *(Edward and Charlotte enter, arm in arm — each in a buoyant mood. Charlotte carries the small wooden box from the prologue.)*

CHARLOTTE. Do you see, Nicolas, how the country suits her? She is very happy here.

EDWARD. We all are — it's a day of celebration!

CHARLOTTE. Listen to you! You've never cared for "festivities" before.

EDWARD. I love them now! I am a new man! But, where is the Captain — it's nearly time! *(Edward moves away, looking for the Captain, as — Mittler enters, carrying an object on a tripod, and a weathered leather satchel. Trailing him, playfully, is Lucianne.)*

MITTLER. I come not as a celebrant, but as a *witness*! By christening this pavilion today do you, Charlotte and Edward, proclaim to the world: "Here is the place from whence we shall view the future together." *(Mittler sets up the object he has brought —)* And, to that end, I will capture this day in the lens of my *camera obscura*.

OTTILIE. *(Going to him, curious.)* A *camera obscura* — what is that?

LUCIANNE. *(With a worldly laugh.)* Oh, haven't you seen one?

MITTLER. It captures a frozen image in this dark chamber, then projects it onto a flat surface.

NICOLAS. Then, he will sketch the outline with a pencil — and have a record of the moment.

OTTILIE. That is remarkable.

LUCIANNE. In the *city* they are *everywhere*.

CHARLOTTE. Ottilie, Lucianne — I need your help. *(Ottilie and Lucianne help Charlotte with some final decorations, as — Mittler continues setting up his equipment, and — Nicolas approaches Edward.)*

NICOLAS. Those poplars in the distance … quite majestic.

EDWARD. *(Matter-of-fact.)* Not for long. The lake — once it expands — will swallow them forever. Nature, you see, shares your gift for persistence.

NICOLAS. By that, you mean —

EDWARD. Your letters to Ottilie arrive with such regularity. And

55

the penmanship on the envelope — quite *artful*, quite … *feminine*, really.

NICOLAS. I wish only to inquire about her well-being.

EDWARD. She seldom reads them, you know. Oh, they warm her day — make no mistake — but, then she laughs and says "Oh, Nicolas" — and tosses them into the fire. *(Edward turns and looks out at the vista.)*

NICOLAS. I'm glad she's so content.

EDWARD. That she is.

NICOLAS. For an orphan girl to find a home is a wonderful thing.

EDWARD. She seldom speaks of her family.

NICOLAS. Perhaps because her family is *here.*

EDWARD. *(Pause.)* Yes.

NICOLAS. Charlotte sees to her education, I'm sure.

EDWARD. Yes, she does.

NICOLAS. And you … I'm sure Ottilie is glad to have found such a *father-figure. (Nicolas leaves Edward, as — Charlotte calls to him —)*

CHARLOTTE. Edward, the Count and Baroness should be here by now.

MITTLER. *(With sudden anger.)* BLASPHEMY!

CHARLOTTE. *(Firmly, to Mittler.)* They've been our dear friends for years, and are welcome here as our guests.

MITTLER. I had no idea that such a *contagion* would be arriving in our midst.

LUCIANNE. *(Deliciously, to Ottilie.)* The Count and the Baroness sneak away to the country each summer to be together. The state will not grant either of them a divorce from their *loveless, suffocating, pre-arranged* marriages — so they are *trapped! C'est merveilleux, n'est-ce pas? (The Count and the Baroness enter, arm in arm — impeccably dressed, delighted to be together. The Baroness carries the parasol she used in the Prologue.)*

THE COUNT. What a remarkable sight!

MITTLER. Oh, rue the day …

THE COUNT. The endless vista before us and our dear friends around us!

| EDWARD. | CHARLOTTE. | LUCIANNE. |
| Welcome! | And here you are! | Look at them. |

THE BARONESS. *(Embracing them both.)* Oh, Charlotte — the estate and its lady are more beautiful than ever! And Edward — still setting hearts aflutter!

CHARLOTTE. I believe you know my niece, Lucianne.

LUCIANNE. *Un plaisir de vous voir encore une fois.*

THE COUNT. *(Smitten.)* How could one forget her?

LUCIANNE. *(Taking Nicolas by the arm.)* And this is Nicolas, my *beau.*

NICOLAS. I am, rather, her schoolmaster.

CHARLOTTE. And this is our young friend, Ottilie.

LUCIANNE. *(Sweetly.)* She's their *housekeeper.*

THE BARONESS. A pleasure to meet you.

CHARLOTTE. *(Gesturing toward Mittler.)* And, of course, you've met —

MITTLER. *Please don't.* People of such morals should not be introduced — they should be *quarantined.*

THE COUNT. *(Unbowed by Mittler's opinion.)* Your wish has been granted! We are — for the greater part of each year — quarantined within the cruel confines of heartless marriages.

CHARLOTTE. Gentlemen, please —

MITTLER. Marriage is the pinnacle of all man's achievements!

THE COUNT. I wonder if your wife would say the same.

LUCIANNE. He has no wife.

CHARLOTTE. Lucianne —

LUCIANNE. Well, it's true — he doesn't.

MITTLER. I am fully devoted to my *profession* — and *it alone.*

THE BARONESS. You are fully devoted, sir — but only *half aware.* Here before you stand Edward and Charlotte — who once found themselves in the same position as the Count and I.

MITTLER. But they *never requested a divorce.* Their spouses each met untimely deaths.

THE BARONESS. That is my point: they were *lucky.* Death did for them what Fate could not.

CHARLOTTE. This is not a discussion our young people should be hearing.

THE COUNT. And why not?!

MITTLER. Indeed — why not?! Let them learn that those who bemoan their marriage are seeking not a divorce from their spouse

57

— but from their *conscience.*

EDWARD.   CHARLOTTE.   THE BARONESS.
Mittler, please —   You've made your —   You have no right to —

MITTLER. *(Soaring now.)* They want the state to *sanction their unhappiness* and *wipe the guilt of failure from their minds.*

THE COUNT. *(Face to face with Mittler.)* Were you worthy of my glove, sir, I should *slap you. (Mittler immediately turns to Ottilie and Nicolas.)*

MITTLER. Learn this while you are young: marriage is a pact made with eternity. *It cannot be undone. (The Captain enters, happily, wearing his full military uniform. He is carrying a scroll of parchment which has been decorated with ribbons and wildflowers.)*

THE CAPTAIN. Sorry for the delay. But I think now we're — *(He stops.)* Is something wrong?

EDWARD. Everything is fine. And when darkness falls, we have a surprise awaiting us.

CHARLOTTE. What surprise?

EDWARD. You'll see. Now, Captain … *(The Captain climbs atop the platform, where he is flanked by Edward and Charlotte. The others gather around him, watching.)*

THE CAPTAIN. We are here today as witnesses to an earnest labor, conceived by a man and a woman, and dedicated to the contentment of all those they hold dear. For as true friends hold to one another in good times and in bad, so, too, this pavilion shall hold fast to the hillside, in fair weather and in foul, bound not only by the strength of its construction, but by the pure hearts and goodwill of its inhabitants. *(The Captain nods to Lucianne. She pulls the fabric away, revealing the beautifully carved cornerstone of the planned pavilion.)*

EVERYONE. *(As it suits them.)* Here, here. Oh, my … Congratulations. To Edward and Charlotte! Look at that! *C'est épatant!*

THE CAPTAIN. A cornerstone is the soul of a building. And like our own soul, it must be prepared to face eternity. In that spirit, an opening has been carved into this stone, allowing for the placement of items which shall mark this blessed day in time. For my part, I've noted the events of this day on parchment, which I shall place inside. *(The Captain hands the scroll to Edward who places it inside the back [unseen] side of the cornerstone, as —)*

NICOLAS. I've brought wine of this year's vintage. May it be enjoyed on this hillside many years hence. *(Cheers/applause/ad-libs, as — Nicolas hands a bottle of wine to Charlotte who places it inside the cornerstone, as —)*

THE BARONESS. A few coins — recently minted.

THE CAPTAIN. Very good. They, too, shall mark the year. *(The Baroness hands the coins to Edward who places them inside the cornerstone, as — The Count holds up an impressive ring —)*

THE COUNT. This ring.

LUCIANNE.   CHARLOTTE.
It's so beautiful …   Oh, my …

THE COUNT. The ring which I have, for many years, hoped to place on the finger of my beloved. *(With a quick glance to Mittler.)* Since the laws of the present have proven to be an obstacle … I make this vow to the *future*, where surely our two lives will some day be made one. *(Looking at the Baroness, the Count kisses the ring — then hands it to Charlotte who places it inside the cornerstone, as —)*

LUCIANNE.   NICOLAS.   MITTLER.
C'est si romantique!   A very good wish.   BLASPHEMY!

CHARLOTTE. And Lucianne — what about you?

LUCIANNE. *(Desperately.)* Oh, no — I've brought nothing with me. These rituals are so confounding!

THE CAPTAIN. I will contribute something on your behalf. *(The Captain removes a medallion from the chest or shoulder of his uniform, saying —)* This medallion commemorates a battle near the town where your mother and Charlotte were born. I thank God for our victory there, and for the grace by which my own life was spared. *(The Captain hands the medallion to Charlotte, who notices something on the back of it.)*

OTTILIE. And I offer this locket. Like the Captain, I will its contents to the future. *(Ottilie hands the locket, still on its chain, to Edward.)*

EDWARD. *(Aside.)* And there inside the locket was my own image, drawn by her very hand.

CHARLOTTE. *(Aside.)* And as the others looked on, I saw the words which the Captain had inscribed upon the back: "For Charlotte. Forever." *(As Ottilie and the Captain face them — Edward stands, looking down at the open locket — and Charlotte stands next to him, looking down at the medallion.)*

THE COUNT. *(To Edward and Charlotte.)* And what of the two of you?

NICOLAS.	THE BARONESS.	LUCIANNE.
Yes.	Don't be shy.	It's your turn.

THE COUNT. What will you place inside the stone? *(Edward and Charlotte turn and look at each other.)*

CHARLOTTE. *(Quietly.)* I place only my hopes.

EDWARD. As do I. *(Edward and Charlotte place the locket and medallion [respectively] inside the cornerstone, as — Mittler — who has removed the glass chalice from the wooden case — pours some wine into it.)*

MITTLER. One thing more before we compose the tableau. *(A burst of simultaneous responses —)*

THE COUNT.	LUCIANNE.	NICOLAS.
Pose for the what?	Oh, I can't wait!	A *camera obscura* —
THE CAPTAIN.	EDWARD.	CHARLOTTE.
Oh, not again.	Mittler, please —	Oh, yes, the glass.

MITTLER. To christen any structure requires a drink from a crystal cup — *(Mittler hands the chalice to Edward — who drinks the liquid in one long gulp.)*

EVERYONE. *(Cheers/applause/ad-libs.)*

MITTLER. — Followed by the destruction of the glass!

EDWARD. The what?

MITTLER. Only then will good fortune smile upon this place.

EDWARD. But this is the chalice of my boyhood — it's *irreplaceable.*

MITTLER. Suit yourself.

THE COUNT.	LUCIANNE.
Give it here — I'll throw it!	Edward — you must … *(Laughter.)*

EDWARD. But it's a foolish superstition!

MITTLER. If you wish to bring a curse upon this pavilion, be my guest. *(Edward turns looks to the others, who wait, expectantly — He steps to the edge of the platform — Looks into the distance — Then throws the chalice away and out of sight, as — music begins to play.)*

EVERYONE. *(Loud cheers/big applause/ad-libs. Everyone shakes the hands of Edward, Charlotte, and each other — and takes a moment to inspect the cornerstone up close, etc. — as — Mittler readies his camera obscura, and Lucianne climbs atop the platform and gets everyone's attention by exclaiming —*)

LUCIANNE. *Je donnerai chaque personne une place dans le tableau!* The tableau is a magnificent art form and we shall now create one of our very own!

EVERYONE. *(Laughter/cheers/ad-libs in French/good-natured grumbling. Music continues, under, as — during the following, Lucianne quickly gives everyone their place in the tableau — which is situated in an identical manner to the photo in the Prologue. Mittler places his camera obscura in a downstage position, facing them.)*

LUCIANNE. *(Putting Edward and Charlotte in place.)* Our story revolves around a loving married couple and their day of great joy!

THE CAPTAIN.	NICOLAS.	THE BARONESS.
Here, here!	Hooray!	To our hosts!

LUCIANNE. *(Putting the Captain in place next to Charlotte.)* At their side is their loyal friend, the Captain!

EDWARD.	THE COUNT.
We are in his debt.	The bravest of the brave.

LUCIANNE. *(Putting the Count and Baroness in place.)* Also here to mark the day are persons of noble birth with a flair for daring assignations!

CHARLOTTE.	NICOLAS.	MITTLER.
To our friends.	Congratulations!	BLASPHEMY!

LUCIANNE. *(Putting Nicolas in place.)* And what celebration is complete without the handsome young schoolmaster — who decorates the dreams of young women far and wide!

THE CAPTAIN.	THE BARONESS.	CHARLOTTE.
Oh, to be young.	Look at that face …	That's you, Nicolas!

(Edward sees Ottilie standing alone, away from the others.)

EDWARD. Don't forget Ottilie.

LUCIANNE. Oh, yes. *(Putting Ottilie in place, away from Nicolas.)* Every house needs a servant girl to tidy things up.

CHARLOTTE.	NICOLAS.
Lucianne —	She is not a —

(Lucianne now takes her place, on the ground in the forefront of the picture, lying in a beautiful pose near Nicolas —)

LUCIANNE. And finally, in the foreground, a quiet young woman of humble bearing — whose presence completes the

tableau, lifting it from its simple origins and placing it in the hal-
lowed realm of art.

THE BARONESS.   CHARLOTTE.   MITTLER.

Very well done.   That is my niece.   Hold still now —

(They all hold their positions, as Mittler begins sketching the image ...)

THE COUNT. And what do you call this, Lucianne? We must
have a name for our tableau.

LUCIANNE. *(Quietly, beautifully.)* "Un moment parfait en temps."

CHARLOTTE. Yes ...

MITTLER. No one must move ...

LUCIANNE. "A Perfect Moment in Time." *(The instant
Lucianne says this — music stops, abruptly, and — lights isolate the
tableau. The group remains, frozen in place, as Mittler, at a distance,
keeps sketching. Silence for a moment, then, just like Ed in Act One
... Charlotte "steps out" of the tableau, taking in the picture. Looking
back at the others. They do not move. Charlotte then turns and walks
into an area of light downstage.)*

CHARLOTTE. *(Aside.)* Our desire to gather is fundamental.
And, as you know, there is no intimacy greater than that which
takes place in the midst of a crowd. *(A phrase of music, as — the
Count leaves the tableau and approaches Charlotte, purposefully.
Note: Mittler continues to sketch throughout the following scenes.)*

THE COUNT. He is a very impressive man. You are lucky to
have him at your side.

CHARLOTTE. Yes, Edward has always been a —

THE COUNT. I am speaking of the Captain. What a remarkable
piece of work he is! And in light of that, I must ask you a personal question: As regards the Captain, what are your *intentions?*
(Charlotte stares at him.) I am seeking to fill an administrative post
of great distinction. It would afford the rank of major, a consider-
able salary, and other benefits. The Captain, I'm certain, would be
the perfect choice — however, time is of the essence. So, you must
tell me, Charlotte: is your intention to keep him here? Or may I
approach him?

CHARLOTTE. *(Aside, facing the Count.)* You may not have him.
Under no circumstances. He belongs here, right here at my side!
— *(Turning away from the Count.)* — these were the words clam-
oring inside my heart. But all I could utter was — *(End aside, even-*

ly, to the Count.) I have no hold over him.

THE COUNT. Thank you, Charlotte — and please, this must be our secret. *(The Count exits, as — a phrase of music plays, and — the Baroness leaves the tableau, gesturing for Ottilie to join her.)*

THE BARONESS. Ottilie, my dear — may I have a word with you? *(Aside.)* Mature women — even when not fond of one another — maintain an unspoken alliance against beautiful girls.

OTTILIE. What is it, Your Ladyship?

THE BARONESS. *(End aside.)* Have you had a moment to speak with my love, the Count?

OTTILIE. No, I have not.

THE BARONESS. But, still he has been singing your praises. Why would that be? *(Ottilie lowers her head. The Baroness gently lifts Ottilie's chin ... and gently touches her face.)* My intention is not to embarrass you. But to make you *aware*. I fear you possess a power which you do not understand. The Count said not a word to you — but, nevertheless, fell under your spell. Imagine what more *proximate contact* would incite. *(The Baroness holds up a small piece of ribbon or yarn, which has been made into a simple bracelet.)* The knots I've tied into this bracelet — do you know what they're for? *(Ottilie shakes her head, "No.")* They are called "love-knots." This bracelet is worn by a woman who fears her husband is being untrue. The knots, it is said, will render him faithful once again. I'd like you to give this bracelet to Charlotte.

OTTILIE. *(Not taking the bracelet.)* But why? *(The Baroness stares at her. A new tack.)*

THE BARONESS. It's very kind of Charlotte to let you stay here.

OTTILIE. Yes, it is.

THE BARONESS. And how will you repay her?

OTTILIE. I work very hard. I do all she needs of me and more.

THE BARONESS. More?

OTTILIE. Yes.

THE BARONESS. And what might that be?

OTTILIE. I don't understand —

THE BARONESS. Do you like Edward? Do you enjoy his company?

OTTILIE. Yes, of course.

THE BARONESS. He finds you attractive. Do you know that?

(Before Ottilie can respond.) Of course you do. And you find him attractive as well.

OTTILIE. I've not said that.

THE BARONESS. You needn't, my dear. For, you see, it's a truth as old as the world itself: *all attraction is mutual.* You must understand this: Edward and Charlotte are *predestined for one another* — and nothing, or no one, must stand in their way. Is that clear? *(Ottilie is on the verge of tears, as — the Baroness holds out the bracelet and places it into her hands. Ottilie holds it, looking at it, as — the Baroness leads her offstage, saying —)* I think Nicolas is quite the young man, don't you...? *(A phrase of music plays, and — Edward and the Captain emerge from their places in the tableau.)*

EDWARD. *(Urgent, excited.)* Tell me: is everything in place? The fireworks I requested — are they ready to be launched?

THE CAPTAIN. I've stationed a man across the lake. Once darkness falls he will await your signal.

EDWARD. And what is that?

THE CAPTAIN. *(Demonstrating.)* Circle your arm above your head — thus — and the sky shall be filled with color. *(Edward throws his arms around the Captain, avidly.)*

EDWARD. You are my dear friend. And we share a similar secret. I have been consumed by a great passion — and so have you!

THE CAPTAIN. Edward, I have no idea what you are —

EDWARD. You are in love with Charlotte — and we must let nothing stand in your way. If her love matches your own then we are *doubly blessed.* We shall all of us be the happiest people on earth! *(The Captain grabs Edward by the shoulders, forcefully —)*

THE CAPTAIN. Listen to yourself! Do you have any idea what you're saying?

EDWARD. *(Fiercely.)* We are captives, my friend. Caught in the web of an affinity — a force for which our idle, aching hearts are no match. Gravity is as *nothing* — the sun and moon mere *trinkets* — compared with the awesome power which now drives our days.

THE CAPTAIN. But what you are proposing, Edward, it is *wrong.* It is not meant to be.

EDWARD. *According to whom?!* This destiny is placed in our own hands for a reason — and soon we shall affect its completion —

THE CAPTAIN. Edward, no!

EDWARD. Tomorrow shall hear our proposals — tonight is for celebration! *(He does the "fireworks signal" — circling his arm above his head — and he leaves, saying —)* Look to the sky, Captain! Tonight our hearts shall burst into fire! To the sky, my friend, look to the sky! *(Edward rushes away and is gone. A phrase of music plays, and — Nicolas breaks from the tableau and approaches the Captain, with purpose, as — Lucianne looks on.)*

NICOLAS. Pardon me, Captain — but it's urgent that I speak to you.

THE CAPTAIN. *(Distracted.)* Not now —

NICOLAS. But I'm concerned about Ottilie's well-being. As Edward's best friend, I wondered if you could speak to him. There is madness in the air, and I fear —

THE CAPTAIN. Let it be, friend. There is nothing I can do for you — *(The Captain rushes off, as — Lucianne approaches Nicolas.)*

LUCIANNE. Isn't it grand? The way the air grows thick with secrets when we are all together. The way our scheming hearts crash silently here — *(Touching his heart.)* — and there. *(Touching his face, quietly.)* Tell me a secret. One little secret before it grows too large and swallows you whole.

NICOLAS. I can't —

LUCIANNE. You're worried about Ottilie. I have great influence over Charlotte, my aunt — perhaps I can convey your worries to her. *(Silence, as Nicolas looks at her, considering.)* But, first, you must tell me. *Quel est votre sécret?*

NICOLAS. Ottilie was meant to live here.

LUCIANNE. And so she does.

NICOLAS. No, not as a guest — as a *daughter*. Her mother's dying wish was that Charlotte and Edward adopt her as their own. But of the three of them, only Charlotte knows this.

LUCIANNE. *(With a smile.)* Only Charlotte ... and Nicolas ... and Lucianne. *(Pause.)* You're afraid, aren't you?

NICOLAS. What?

LUCIANNE. *Ca va. Je comprends.*

NICOLAS. Lucianne —

LUCIANNE. *(Whispers.)* Let me help you. Let me help you conquer this fear. *(She kisses him — very gently — on the lips. He is seemingly frozen in place.)* I can taste it, you know. *(She licks his lip very*

65

slowly with her tongue.) I can taste the terror on your lips. *(Kisses him.)* It's *delicious. (Nicolas now returns her kiss for a moment, then begins to falter, to back away, but — Lucianne holds him with her arms, forcefully.)* Be brave, Nicolas. Don't run from your fears — be brave. Show me the courage I deserve — *(She leans forward to kiss him once again, but — He pulls away, saying —)*

NICOLAS. Let go of me — *(— and Lucianne falls to the ground, crying out —)*

LUCIANNE. NICOLAS!

NICOLAS. Lucianne, I'm sorry —

LUCIANNE. *(A haunted, heartbreaking rage.)* GO TO HER! TAKE HER HAND AND NEVER COME NEAR ME AGAIN! BUT, BE WARNED, NICOLAS — I WILL MAKE YOU REGRET WHAT YOU'VE DONE — ! *(Lucianne runs off, as — Nicolas chases after her, calling out —)*

NICOLAS. LUCIANNE — ! LUCIANNE — ! *(Mittler watches them go, then moves downstage, holding a small placard on which he has sketched the image of the tableau, as — Ottilie enters.)*

OTTILIE. Have they all gone?

MITTLER. No. They are *here. (He puts the sketch into Ottilie's hands.)* Never forget: *you hold them all in your hands. (Music, as lights shift to —)*

A Bench. Sunset.

In the deep orange glow of sunset, Charlotte and the Captain sit on either end of the small bench. They are each looking at the landscape around them. Each of them is barefoot, with their hosiery removed or rolled up. Their shoes sit beside them on the bench. On her wrist, Charlotte wears the knotted bracelet given to her by the Baroness. Music gives way to the faint sound of gurgling water which underscores the scene. A long moment passes, then ...

THE CAPTAIN. It's a lovely bench.

CHARLOTTE. Thank you. *(Silence.)* It will be a very impressive lake.

THE CAPTAIN. Thank you. *(Silence.)*

CHARLOTTE. How much longer, do you think — before where we sit is completely submerged?

THE CAPTAIN. A few days. A week, at most. *(Pause.)* We could move the bench to dry land — before the water covers it.

CHARLOTTE. No. I will enjoy knowing it's here. Whenever I look at the lake, I will remember this day ... when you and I sat here together. *(Silence.)* You've been avoiding me.

THE CAPTAIN. You are a married woman with an impeccable reputation. I resolved, therefore, to curtail all but the most necessary contact with you.

CHARLOTTE. I thank you for that.

THE CAPTAIN. By all means.

CHARLOTTE. But it did not have the desired effect. Your absence merely heightened my respect for you and that served to compound my attraction. Your plan to temper my affection has been a complete failure.

THE CAPTAIN. I'm sorry. *(Silence. They look at the landscape, at the water beginning to surround them.)*

CHARLOTTE. Soon we shall need a boat.

THE CAPTAIN. I've ordered one. The finest of its kind — it will arrive next week. The mark of a well-made boat is that one person can row it alone.

CHARLOTTE. How comforting. *(Silence.)*

THE CAPTAIN. What is that on your wrist?

CHARLOTTE. It is from the Baroness. To ward off impropriety. Though it seems the Count has a more tangible plan.

THE CAPTAIN. I was hoping you wouldn't release me from my work.

CHARLOTTE. And I was hoping you'd decline his offer. But you haven't, have you?

THE CAPTAIN. I shall be leaving in the morning. *(Silence. Then — Charlotte holds her hand at some distance from her face, fingers spread, staring at her palm.)*

CHARLOTTE. Look at the lines. So recklessly etched into us. A page folded in a book, and then forgotten. *(As she continues to look at her hand, the Captain reaches out his hand and puts it in hers. When his hand meets hers ... her eyes close.)* Love is for the young. It is a bond made in the ascending years of our life ... as a way of comforting us on our descent. *(Turning, looking in his eyes.)* So, what am I to make of *this*? I resent the *inelegance* of it. To find you now is an indictment of my own past. You are the proof of how much life I have wasted.

THE CAPTAIN. *(Quietly.)* I will do whatever you ask. But I am powerless to alter these feelings.

CHARLOTTE. *(Also quietly.)* Then we must alter our lives. *(Pause.)* I shall imagine you far away, in a fine home befitting your new rank of Major. I shall envision you properly married to a woman of stature and grace. *(She releases her hand from his.)* I shall see her hand in yours. *(Calmly, surely.)* And I shall renounce you. Utterly and completely. I shall fall to my knees and renew my vow to Edward. And in doing so ... I shall be restored. *(Charlotte stands, takes a few steps away from the bench and looks out at the approaching water.)* For you see, I, too can affect the world. *(She picks up a small stone from the ground. Looks at it in her hand.)* I can toss this stone into the water — and the force of its fall will ripple out and reach the far side of this valley. And then ... in time ... everything, blessedly, will be calm once again. *(Charlotte prepares to throw the stone, saying —)* I need only — *(But she is interrupted by Nicolas who rushes on, desperately, and pulls the Captain to his feet during the following —)*

NICOLAS. Captain — you must come — !

THE CAPTAIN. What is it?

NICOLAS. It's Lucianne — she was walking along the top ridge of the dam — I begged her not to — I told her it was not safe up there — but she didn't listen — !

THE CAPTAIN.	CHARLOTTE.
And what happened?	Nicolas, calm down —

NICOLAS. Some of the earth gave way — and she fell into the water below — *we can't reach her — she's trapped —*

CHARLOTTE. Oh, my —

NICOLAS. YOU MUST COME — *(Nicolas rushes off, followed by the Captain. Charlotte looks down at the stone in her hands, as lights shift to —)*

The Hillside. Evening.

Edward rushes on, pulling Ottilie by the hand.

EDWARD. Ottilie! Wait!

OTTILIE. Edward — we must go to her!

EDWARD. *(Riding a wave of emotions.)* We're too far away — we'd have to cross the entire lake —

OTTILIE. But the others may need our help —

EDWARD. Ottilie, listen: Lucianne is safe in their loving hands — just as we are held in the hands of Destiny!

OTTILIE. What are you saying?!

EDWARD. Look at this! *(Edward reaches into his coat and removes the chalice which he threw down the hillside. It shines, unblemished.)* The chalice — it is unbroken! It was spared by the limbs of a tree which caught and protected it.

OTTILIE. That is a terrible omen. Mittler said it *must break* — to bring good fortune to us all, he said it —

EDWARD. No — you must look. You must look closely — *(He shows her the letters inscribed on the chalice.)* An "O" and an "E" — *intertwined and unbroken!* You are right, Ottilie, it is an omen — a *blessed one!* "Ottilie" and "Edward" — together, complete and inseparable! *(She holds the chalice in her hands, looking at it, as Edward turns quickly to the audience — aside, in a fury.)* It is wrong to be here and I know that. On any other day of my life I would be with the others, giving aid — but, don't you see: *She is a comet which shall pass my life but once* — and I must speak my heart now or live my regret forever.

OTTILIE. I made a vow, Edward. That I would do nothing to disrupt the tranquillity of your home —

EDWARD. *(End aside.) Am I alone in this love?* That is the only question that matters.

OTTILIE. Your marriage to Charlotte — you are predestined for one another —

EDWARD. That destiny was but prelude to this one!

OTTILIE. But, I have no right to come between you —

EDWARD. *All rights vanish before the rights of love!* We are bound by nothing but the sky and the stars —

OTTILIE. Edward, we must join the others —

EDWARD. All of history — each conquest and discovery, each sonnet and song — was but prelude to *this moment!*

OTTILIE. Edward, please — *(Edward looks across the vista and waves his arm wildly above his head, signaling —)*

EDWARD. LET THE HEAVENS ALIGHT IN YOUR HONOR! *(Music, joined by — a loud cacophony of explosions which ring out, and an array of lights which bedevil the stage and sky, as — Ottilie, terrified, shrinks to the ground.)* Rockets and fireballs — roaring and bursting into the sky!

OTTILIE. Edward, I'm afraid —

EDWARD. But these are the fireworks I promised you! Roman candles and fiery serpents and the spinning of the Catherine wheel — look at them all!

OTTILIE. Please — make them stop —

EDWARD. But they are for you! *(The music reaches a crescendo — the fireworks explode with abandon, as Ottilie stands and rushes off —)*

OTTILIE. No — they must stop — !

EDWARD. *(Calling after her.)* OTTILIE — YOU MUST LOOK AT THEM — THEY ARE ALL FOR YOU! *(Music continues, under, as lights shift quickly to a separate area —)*

The Grounds of the Estate. Night.

The Captain enters, carrying Lucianne in his arms. Their clothing is torn and wet. They are followed by Charlotte, the Count, the Baroness, and Nicolas — who is carrying a lantern. A tone of urgency prevails.

THE COUNT. The Captain has saved her life. I saw it with my own eyes — *(Charlotte helps the Captain place a blanket around the shivering Lucianne.)*

NICOLAS. Her breathing is restored —

THE BARONESS. God be thanked —

THE COUNT. The man leapt from the dam and into the water —

THE CAPTAIN. Just a moment's rest, then we must take her to the house —

THE COUNT. — And by his own hand freed her from the rocks below.

THE BARONESS. She is a lucky girl.

NICOLAS. *(Kneeling next to her.)* I fear this is my fault. Lucianne was upset with me, and she — *(Lucianne now opens her eyes, lifts her hand and places her fingers gently against Nicolas' mouth, quieting him, as — the distant sounds of explosions are heard, and — they all look up to the sky, as — multi-colored light begins to color their faces.)*

THE COUNT. What is that sound? *(Charlotte stands and looks into the distance.)*

THE BARONESS. Charlotte?

CHARLOTTE. *(Simply, looking to the sky.)* As promised, Edward has surprised us all. *(Now, Charlotte walks slowly downstage amid the noise. As she does so, lights shift, and —)*

The Drawing Room. Night.

— is assembled around her. Charlotte goes to the table — where a half-dozen leather-bound journals are stacked — and she opens one of them, as — Edward appears at a distance. His clothing suggests he has come directly from the fireworks on the hillside.

EDWARD. How is Lucianne?

CHARLOTTE. She is resting. A doctor has been sent for.

EDWARD. Thank goodness the Captain was here.

CHARLOTTE. Yes. But tomorrow he shall be gone.

EDWARD. Is that so?

CHARLOTTE. And what of us, Edward? Shall we return to our former life? Or shall we come to a new arrangement? *(Aside.)* And yes, of course, I am *testing him*. I now expect from others the same *self-control* which has been demanded of *me*.

EDWARD. My wish is to know your thoughts.

CHARLOTTE. *(End aside.)* I find our current status unacceptable.

EDWARD. As do I.

CHARLOTTE. Then we are agreed.

EDWARD. *(Hopeful.)* Yes — it's remarkable — I believe we share an identical wish.

CHARLOTTE. We must be *clear*, Edward — each to the other.

EDWARD. I agree completely!

CHARLOTTE. Very well. I shall speak to Ottilie tonight. *(Going to him.)* This reflects well on you, Edward. That you are willing to make this sacrifice for our happiness.

EDWARD. *(Confused.)* What are you saying?

CHARLOTTE. She will be sent back to the boarding school, back to her —

EDWARD. But, you can't expect Ottilie to leave us.

CHARLOTTE. I do not expect it — I *demand* it!

EDWARD. But, at one time you wished only for her happiness — don't you see that I now share that wish?!

CHARLOTTE. You have shared more than that. *(She moves to the journals on the table.)* Your travel journals. I found them in Ottilie's room.

EDWARD. I've given her permission to read them.

CHARLOTTE. She is *illustrating them*. In her own hand. She is traveling with you, page after page, sketching the scenes as you describe them — living the part of your life which was promised to me.

EDWARD. But, to send her away — must we go to such extremes?!

CHARLOTTE. This *passion* is extreme! And *we both must fight it!* It has infected us and soon will consume us.

EDWARD. *(Aside.)* And a dreadful thing happened —

CHARLOTTE. We are no longer children.

EDWARD. *(Aside.)* The most dreadful thing of all —

CHARLOTTE. We are responsible for one another.

EDWARD. *(Aside.)* I knew in my heart that she was *right*.

CHARLOTTE. Now, please — *help me*.

EDWARD. *(Aside.)* So, naturally, I grew more adamant in my refusal.

CHARLOTTE. I can't face this alone.

EDWARD. *(End aside, suddenly.)* Then let the Captain be at your side. I release you to him — that your journey with him may bring you the life I failed to provide.

CHARLOTTE. *(Aside.)* And a terrible thing happened.

EDWARD. Let others call it mischief or folly, let their tongues wag in gossip and dissent — we shall pay them no mind.

CHARLOTTE. *(Aside.)* The most terrible thing of all —

EDWARD. *We must answer to no one but our own hearts.*

CHARLOTTE. *(Aside.)* He was *right*. He was granting me the full power of my hopes — and for a moment I saw it all before me … my new life, with the Captain at my side. I was *this close* to embracing that life … but then I looked in Edward's eyes — *(She does, pause.)* — and I grew not *weak* … but something worse, something much harder to overcome … I grew *proud*. I refused to lose him to another. Even to a woman I loved. I refused to relinquish my rights to him — even if it meant abandoning my own happiness. *(End aside, quietly.)* I will not give you up. *(Silence. The tone begins to shift to cold negotiation.)*

EDWARD. We each then have made a sacrifice.

CHARLOTTE. Yes.

EDWARD. And thus each should be allowed a demand.

CHARLOTTE. I have made mine. I demand an end to your time with Ottilie.

EDWARD. And I shall see to that.

CHARLOTTE. Thank you. *(Silence. Edward closes his journal.)* And you, Edward? What is your demand?

EDWARD. *(Aside.)* And the first thought that came to mind — *(End aside.)* That Ottilie stay here with you. I want to know that she is safe and well-cared for.

CHARLOTTE. I don't understand.

EDWARD. I must leave this place, Charlotte. I don't know where

I'll go — but, only distance will cure this affliction. As for Ottilie, I shall make no attempt to contact her *as long as she is with you.* If you send her away, however, I shall consider our agreement broken — and I shall know that you've consented to let her be mine. *(Aside.)* And she said nothing. And we stood there ... our great love, our life together racing even then into the past. *(Edward leaves, as a shaft of light isolates — Charlotte, alone. Music plays under.)*

CHARLOTTE. *(Aside.)* The next morning, I was awakened by the sound of horses. I rushed to my window, and I saw not Edward leaving — but the Captain. *(A silhouette of the Captain is seen upstage.)* I pressed my hands to the glass, praying he would turn and see me — but, ever the soldier, he never once looked back. I watched him ride ... past the lake and its relentless, ever-rising water ... I watched him till I was watching nothing but the absence of him. And a pain — a pain that my body had never known — shot through me like fire. *(A shaft of light isolates Ottilie, opposite. On the ground in front of her is a beautiful wooden chest. She lifts a letter from atop the chest and reads from it, as — a silhouette of Edward is seen upstage, opposite the Captain. Charlotte remains lit, staring front.)*

OTTILIE. *(Reads.)* "My dear Ottilie: This is called a hope chest. I have filled it with clothing and linens and other finery — as befits your beauty and grace. It also holds — quite literally, I'm afraid — my own hopes. I entrust them to your loving, caring hands."

CHARLOTTE. *(Aside.)* How is the heart made, I wonder?

OTTILIE. "Remember me ... "

CHARLOTTE. *(Aside.)* How does it ache so deeply at the loss of something it has never known? *(Music fades, and lights expand downstage to reveal —)*

The Drawing Room. Day.

Charlotte and Ottilie each approach the table and sit, facing each other. Their demeanor is courteous and contrite. The other two chairs are conspicuously empty. Charlotte works at her ledger. Ottilie makes drawings inside Edward's travel journals.

OTTILIE. *(Quietly.)* How long has it been? Since they left?
CHARLOTTE. Nearly two months.
OTTILIE. Do you think they'll ever return? Either of them?
CHARLOTTE. You asked that very question yesterday. *(Pause.)* I've no idea. *(Silence. They return to their work.)*
OTTILIE. The lake is full now. The entire park covered over.
CHARLOTTE. Yes.
OTTILIE. How strong must that dam be? To hold back a force such as that. *(Pause, as they work.)* I saw the doctor here this morning. Are you feeling ill?
CHARLOTTE. I shall be fine. *(Aside.)* And in this manner, weeks passed. I tended to the business of the estate. Ottilie filled Edward's travel journals with drawings, as I sat only a glance away. From time to time, a few words would be exchanged — and then … once again … stillness. Avoidance. And sweet gloom. There is nothing so loud as the silence of a common longing. Even the visits of our friends did little to distract us — *(Music, as a shaft of light isolates — The Count and the Baroness, more buoyant than ever. Charlotte and Ottilie do not look up.)*
THE BARONESS. The gods have smiled on us at last!
THE COUNT. My wife succumbed to a fever, and her husband was shot and killed in a duel!
THE BARONESS. Our prayers have been answered!
THE COUNT. And now —
THE BARONESS. After a suitable period of mourning, of course —

THE COUNT. Of course —

THE BARONESS. We can finally be joined together as husband and wife!

THE COUNT. And love each other without fear of reprisal!

THE BARONESS. Isn't that wonderful?!

THE COUNT. By the way, about that *ring* I left at your estate...! *(Music fades, as — the Baroness laughs, and pulls the Count out of the light, and they are gone.)*

CHARLOTTE. *(Quietly, kindly.)* Ottilie?

OTTILIE. Yes?

CHARLOTTE. The hope chest which Edward gave you ... you've never opened it.

OTTILIE. No.

CHARLOTTE. But, why?

OTTILIE. *(Desperate, fearful.)* Teach me to renounce him. To renounce Edward as you did the Captain. *(Charlotte closes her ledger. Looks at Ottilie. After a long silence ...)*

CHARLOTTE. *(Aside, gently.)* And, of course, I could not. *(Aside, stroking Ottilie's hair, tenderly.)* The decision of one heart offers no precedent for another. *(Ottilie stands and goes, as — Mittler rushes on.)* Mittler — I expected you months ago.

MITTLER. I am fully informed about your situation.

CHARLOTTE. Then why haven't you come?! When finally we needed your help —

MITTLER. *(Enjoying this.)* You are the sort of people who constantly believe that Fate will cure your ills, that Destiny will restore order to your life. *Well?* Has everything *fallen into place* and *worked out for the best?!*

CHARLOTTE. You needn't mock me, sir —

MITTLER. I will *mock* you until you allow me to *help you!*

CHARLOTTE. We are in disarray. We each await Edward's return — but do not know when it will come ... or for whom he is returning.

MITTLER. What a preposterous arrangement!

CHARLOTTE. You are wise about marriage, sir — but you've no understanding of love.

MITTLER. It is not *love* that has led you astray, but *idleness* — a *capricious disregard* for —

CHARLOTTE. *Please. A truce.* Believe me, I should love to have the idle heart you accuse me of — for mine is full of motion, a torn sail rippling in the wind.

MITTLER. He is in France. *(Charlotte turns to him.)* He has spent months wandering aimlessly in the countryside. I shall go in search of him. And when I find him, I shall appeal to his sense of duty — and when that fails (which is generally the case). I shall appeal to his *vanity.* I will report to him on the groundswell of innuendo which is tarnishing his good name — and bringing disgrace to the noble title of "Husband."

CHARLOTTE. *(Quietly.)* And Father. *(Mittler stares at her, as — Charlotte places her hands on her abdomen.)* I still believe, you see. I still believe that all can be restored. For what means this child, if not as a sign that Edward will return to me and we shall renew our life together?

MITTLER. And the child — if you'll pardon the indelicacy of my question — is the child…?

CHARLOTTE. Edward's own. Yes. We have hoped for this since the day we were married. But such hopes were barren … until now. Is that not a miracle?

MITTLER. *(Ecstatic.)* In all of my matrimonial arsenal is there no argument greater than this: that *Nature itself has formed a bond between you. (Mittler rushes off, joyously —)*

CHARLOTTE. But, sir —

MITTLER. Farewell! *(Music plays, as lights shift to —)*

A Rock Wall. Day.

This is, in actuality, the back side of the dam. Ottilie stands at the base of the wall, holding a large piece of chalk in her hand. She also holds a white cloth rag. She is marking the wall with chalk — completing a large drawing. Lucianne sits on a stone, nearby, angled to face Ottilie. She is holding the sketch which Mittler made, so that Ottilie can see it, and draw from it. Music fades.

OTTILIE. I live in my imagination now. With Edward gone, there is not a place for me in the world.

LUCIANNE. And so you come *here?*

OTTILIE. This rock wall holds the force of the entire lake behind it. I find that comforting.

LUCIANNE. *(Lowering the picture.)* It makes me nervous.

OTTILIE. *(Gestures for her to lift the picture.)* And Mittler's picture of us all — it captured our innocence. I seek to transfer it. To enlarge and prolong it.

LUCIANNE. But the rain will wash it away.

OTTILIE. Perhaps. But I will have done what I can to restore order. To summon the tranquillity we have lost.

LUCIANNE. It's a good thing you came to the country. In the city they'd lock you up. *(Ottilie smiles, not taking offense, as — Lucianne looks away.)* Do you ever wish you were dead? *(Ottilie stops working, and looks at her.)* I threw myself from the top of this dam — down into the water.

OTTILIE. But Nicolas said you'd fallen —

LUCIANNE. I didn't fall. He had broken my heart and I wanted to die. Sometimes I still do ... *(Ottilie sets down her chalk and kneels beside Lucianne. Lucianne's voice is quiet and firm.)* I hate that he loves you. That they all love you. Especially Edward, the man who should have been your stepfather. *(Pause, this has slipped out.)* I'm sorry. You never knew? *(Ottilie shakes her head "No.")* It was your Mother's wish — but Charlotte refused to honor it. Even Edward doesn't know. *(Silence.)*

OTTILIE. *(Quietly.)* As you fell into the water ... what did you feel?

LUCIANNE. *(Also quietly.)* I felt free. *(Silence.)*

OTTILIE. Thank you. *(Lucianne turns to her. Ottilie speaks with a calm certainty.)* And, now I know how to renounce him: by making my love for him *completely selfless.* I shall pray not for our future, but only for his well-being ... and his safe return. *(Music, under as lights reveals —)*

A Courtyard. Night.

*All that is required is a high window — identical to the end
of Act One. Edward stands some distance from the window.
He wears a weathered black frock coat. His demeanor is pas-
sionate, lost, intense.*

EDWARD. *(Aside.)* I am adrift upon an ocean of imaginings —
my days but a storm of hope and torment, serenity and tears. And
though I desire nothing but to have her at my side ... I am left,
instead, with only visions ... only dreams. *(Now, gradually visible
in the window, illuminated only by moonlight, is the naked back of a
young woman. She is visible only from the waist up. She is slowly
brushing her beautiful long hair. The image is nearly identical to the
end of Act One. Edward gradually turns and sees the woman as he
speaks. Enraptured.)* I am home at my estate. Wandering through
the lush night like a thief. And yes ... there ... in her window ...
there is Ottilie. And like a tonic — seeing her there in the moonlight simplifies my life to the quick: *I have never loved before.* Only
now do I know that. Everything before her was prologue; every
hour without her, merely pastime, delay. *(Calling to the window.)*
Oh, Ottilie, how this can this be? How can our memories be so
sweet and our future so impossible...? *(On Edward's final word, the
young woman, suddenly aware of his presence, turns quickly — covering her chest with her folded arms, as — Her frightened eyes lock
with Edward's for a quick, charged moment, then — music out, as —
a man's voice, furious, shatters the silence —)*
VOICE OF THE HUSBAND. *Vous, là! (The light on the young
woman snaps out, as — a silhouette of the husband is seen. He is
dressed in black, wearing a hat. We never see his face.) Vous déson-
norez ma femme avec vos regards fixes et lascifs!*
EDWARD. I meant no harm, sir —
THE HUSBAND. *Entrant dans la cour — regardant par sa fen-
etre — at avec quelle intention, monsieur?!*

79

EDWARD. She is but a vision of my loved one — the woman for whom —

THE HUSBAND. Vous m'insultez, monsieur — and je demande une réparation! *(The husband is gone as quickly as he appeared.)*

EDWARD. No, please, wait — *(Aside.)* Two men approached me the next day. For what was being called my "attempted seduction of their master's beloved" — I had been challenged to a duel. One day hence. At dawn. *(Mittler rushes on.)*

MITTLER. And so at last you need my help! I have horses waiting at a secret location. Meet me there at midnight and I shall deliver you from this cabal of civility currently seeking your death. Once home, we shall see to the restoration of your marriage and your sanity.

EDWARD. How did you find me?

MITTLER. *Brilliantly*, if you must know — but there's no time to tell it. You must hide in the woods till midnight, then —

EDWARD. I am not leaving.

MITTLER. What?!

EDWARD. I welcome this duel.

MITTLER. But you know nothing about —

EDWARD. *(At his very edge.) I want danger.* Do you understand?! This man's challenge is a godsend! I welcome this danger from without — for I must counterbalance the danger from *within*.

MITTLER. But, Edward —

EDWARD. I appoint you my second.

MITTLER. I have summoned the Captain. I sent him to your challenger to affect a peaceful resolution.

EDWARD. It is not peace I desire. I wish to court destruction. *(The Captain enters, in a uniform befitting his new rank of Major. He stops when he sees Edward.)*

THE CAPTAIN. Edward.

EDWARD. Mittler tells me you have been negotiating my honor. Please, tell me where it stands.

THE CAPTAIN. To my mind, your honor is intact. It is my own which has been tarnished. Like a coward I left your estate — this my shameful answer to your kind generosity. And never once did I face you and confess my disloyalty. *(Edward steps forward and takes the Captain by the shoulders.)*

EDWARD. Your true, abiding friendship is confession enough. *(The men shake hands, looking into each other's eyes.)*

MITTLER. *(Aside, exasperated.)* Had I but known what a case I was undertaking!

EDWARD. Now, to the duel.

THE CAPTAIN. Your challenger seems to live from one perceived insult to another. This is his third duel in as many weeks.

EDWARD. And, as a marksman, is he —

THE CAPTAIN. Expert. Unerring. Extremely well-versed.

EDWARD. I see.

MITTLER. The entire ritual is nothing but stupidity dressed up as bravery.

THE CAPTAIN. Tell me, have you never insulted a man's honor?!

MITTLER. Many times! But never by *accident!*

EDWARD. The details.

THE CAPTAIN. Your challenger considers this a third level insult, which means it must be settled by pistols. I demanded there be only one round of shots, at a distance of fifteen paces — both of which are standard and fair.

MITTLER. *(Moving away.)* Ghastly — every bit of it …

THE CAPTAIN. What is less ordinary is the "style" he has requested. It is known as "on cue," in which the two men take aim, and then — on a signal of some kind — *both fire at once.*

EDWARD. I accept.

THE CAPTAIN. But Edward, the point of a duel is not to kill, but to make a man *face death* — thereby restoring the honor of both parties —

EDWARD. I accept.

THE CAPTAIN. But the "on cue" provides no chance for personal courage — only random, spontaneous carnage!

EDWARD. It is the most dangerous style, then? The most dependant on sheer *chance*?

THE CAPTAIN. *Completely!*

EDWARD. I *accept.*

MITTLER.	THE CAPTAIN.
No —	Edward —

EDWARD. *(To Mittler.)* Go to the man and convey my thoughts. In this duel shall I place the question of my fate. And tomorrow at dawn I shall have my answer. *(To the Captain.)* Fear nothing, friend. For if I am killed, Charlotte will be free to marry. Thus, one victory between us is assured.

MITTLER. You foolish man. You are fighting for someone else. Someone whose life your actions shall affect forever. *(Edward turns to him.)* Even now — as we bicker over the formalities of death — your wife is preparing to give birth. Let us reverence the moment that joined you to her. May it serve a beacon to bring you to her side once again. *(Edward looks to the Captain, who says nothing. Mittler approaches Edward.)* Edward, I will accept for you this challenge — with one condition: that if you survive the morning, you will return home to your wife, and your child. Are we agreed?

EDWARD. I shall see you at dawn. *(Music under, as lights shift quickly to a downstage corner of the stage which will serve as —)*

Charlotte's Room. Night.

All that is required for this brief scene is a comfortable chair in beautiful light. Charlotte sits in the chair, her pregnancy at full-term. She wears a lovely nightgown. From behind her — Ottilie enters. Charlotte, of course, does not hear her approach. Ottilie moves beside the chair ... and then gently reaches her hand down ... placing it upon Charlotte's womb. Charlotte is not startled. She places her own hands atop Ottilie's — holding them lovingly to her own womb, closing her eyes.

CHARLOTTE. I wonder if my child shall walk as quietly as you.

OTTILIE. *(Quietly.)* When will it happen?

CHARLOTTE. I dreamt that I will give birth at first light. If it's a girl, I'll name her Beatrice — after your mother. *(Ottilie smiles, warmly, at the thought.)*

OTTILIE. And if it's a boy?

CHARLOTTE. *(Quietly.)* Otto.

OTTILIE. After Edward?

CHARLOTTE. Yes. *(Pause.)* After Edward. *(Music fades, and lights shift to —)*

A Field. Dawn.

Mist covers an expanse of the stage, as — Edward enters, walking slowly, purposefully. The Captain walks at his side, carrying a mahogany pistol case. They maintain an even, almost formal tone.

EDWARD. A lovely site. Did you select it?
THE CAPTAIN. The land is flat behind him. That will silhouette him clearly against the sky. I shall take your coat. *(Edward removes his frock coat — revealing a white silk shirt underneath. He places the coat over the Captain's arm. Then, the Captain opens the pistol case and holds it in front of Edward.)* Each have been inspected by both sides. *(Edward nods … and removes a pistol from the case, as the Captain speaks —)* And, if I may advise, place your free arm tightly against your chest — as protection for your heart. *(Edward nods. The Captain produces a white silk handkerchief from a pocket of his coat.)* The signal shall be *the drop of this handkerchief.* Is that clear? *(Edward nods, looking in his eyes.)* God speed, Edward. *(Music begins, under.)*
EDWARD. *(With an odd, quiet manner.)* I awoke this morning to Ottilie's voice. As though she were hovering above me like an angel. *(Music builds, as — the Captain exits, and — Edward readies himself, holding the pistol over his head, standing in profile — facing the audience, where the [unseen] adversary awaits. At the same moment, a shaft of light also reveals —)*

The Rock Wall. Dawn.

Ottilie is there, alone, drawing shapes onto the stone with chalk, as before. Also, as before, she holds a cloth rag in her hand. A man's voice rings out —

MAN'S VOICE. *Preparez-vous! (Edward lowers the gun and takes aim, as — Ottilie makes another mark with her chalk. Edward places his other arm against his chest, covering his heart, as — Ottilie wipes at the chalk mark with her cloth rag. Edward waits, his hand squeezing the pistol tightly, his face one of grim determination — And then, all things seemingly at once: Ottilie casually drops the cloth rag to the ground, and — Edward fires, as — the amplified sound of two gunshots echoes wildly, and — music crescendos, and — all light snaps out, except for —)*

Charlotte's Room. Dawn.

A shaft of light on Charlotte's face as she screams in agony for only a moment, and then — darkness. Silence. Calm.

The Field. Dawn.

Very slowly, a light discovers Edward, collapsed on the ground in the misty, abandoned field. He is weeping, clutching his hands to his chest, as — the Captain rushes on, holding Edward's coat.

THE CAPTAIN. *(Fearful.)* Edward — are you hit? *(Edward does not respond, as — Mittler appears at a distance.)*

EDWARD. *(A desperate joy.)* How long I waited — how far I searched — and now today the voice of Destiny has spoken — *(He quickly reaches into the pocket of his coat – which the Captain still holds — and produces the chalice. He lifts it to the sky, tears streaming down his face. A man reborn.)* Don't you see?! I put my life in the hands of Fate — I resolved to become like this chalice and *make of my own life an omen* — and just as this chalice was spared — so, too, was I!

MITTLER. *(Approaching.)* God be thanked. You can return home, as promised.

EDWARD. *(To the Captain.)* You were right, friend. This duel made me face my own death. And the moment the guns were fired, I knew with certainty *that I am Ottilie's and she is mine.* *(Edward turns to Mittler, forcefully —)* You must help us — Charlotte and I must be divorced.

MITTLER. What are you saying?!

EDWARD. It will do nothing but sanction what is *already in effect.* Charlotte will be free to marry the Captain — and in that way *one divorce* shall produce *two blessed marriages.*

THE CAPTAIN. But, Edward, all has *changed.* Your child is to be born —

MITTLER. — And this child must now influence the whole of our plans!

EDWARD. *(Forcefully, to Mittler.)* Had you the choice to be born into *two happy families* or *one miserable one,* which would you choose? How dare you sentence my child to a life like that! *(Music under, as — Edward turns to the Captain, and a shaft of light reveals — Ottilie, at her hope chest. As Edward speaks — Ottilie kneels at the chest and opens it, slowly, for the first time, and ... light pours up out of the chest, illuminating her face. From the chest, Ottilie slowly lifts a simple, very beautiful white dress. She looks at it, admiring it, then holds it tightly to her chest ...)* As to our reputations and our standing in polite society, I say this: *that the will of four people —* spoken with honesty, heard with compassion, and enacted with care — *shall withstand all the forces of man.* *(The Captain stares at him, then, finally, responds —)*

85

THE CAPTAIN. If Charlotte consents — *and only then* — will I support your plan.

EDWARD. Our future ... I see it all before me. And with such *certainty* — as though it were something *which had already come to pass. music fades, as — Ottilie closes the hope chest, and lights shift to —*)

The Grounds of the Estate. Afternoon.

Charlotte walks on, holding the infant child in her arms. A small wicker basket is on the ground, nearby.

OTTILIE. Only four weeks — and so big, already.

CHARLOTTE. Having you here is a godsend. I couldn't care for him without you.

OTTILIE. *(Gently.)* Of course you could. You are ready now to be a mother. *(Charlotte looks at her.)* When I was a girl, you were not.

CHARLOTTE. Ottilie ...

OTTILIE. Nothing more need be said. We are together now, when we need each other most.

CHARLOTTE. Will you take him with you on your walk?

OTTILIE. Of course. *(Ottilie takes the child from Charlotte, and places him inside the wicker basket, as — the Captain enters. A long silence as Charlotte stares at him, saying nothing. Ottilie turns and sees him —)* Captain. We feared we'd never see you.

THE CAPTAIN. And I the same.

OTTILIE. And what of Edward? Is he safe?

THE CAPTAIN. Safe and well, yes. *(Silence. The Captain and Ottilie seem to be waiting for Charlotte to say something, anything ...)* Charlotte?

CHARLOTTE. Your pavilion is complete. Did you see? And our lake is swollen with water. I often row our boat out to the middle of it ... and there I sit ... imagining my park, submerged for eternity. *(Silence.)*

THE CAPTAIN. Motherhood suits you.

CHARLOTTE. It does, in fact. And he is a remarkable little boy. *(Ottilie brings the child to the Captain.)* I named him Otto.

THE CAPTAIN. *(Pause.)* After Edward? *(Silence. She does not answer.)*

OTTILIE. I was just going for a walk. Excuse me. *(Turns back to the Captain.)* Welcome home. *(Ottilie goes, taking the child with her.)*

CHARLOTTE. Is Edward with you?

THE CAPTAIN. Yes. He asked me to convey his wish to return. *(Silence.)*

CHARLOTTE. I have been thinking of you.

THE CAPTAIN. I'm glad for that.

CHARLOTTE. I feel a man in your position should be married. But … if not … I should like to propose something.

THE CAPTAIN. Yes … in fact, that's why I've come.

CHARLOTTE. I should like to marry you … to Ottilie. I know the effect she had on you when first you met. And now that Edward has returned, Ottilie, I fear, will be the victim of our reunification. *(He looks into her eyes. Speaks, quietly.)*

THE CAPTAIN. Edward has not returned for you. But for her. *(Silence.)*

CHARLOTTE. I see.

THE CAPTAIN. He wishes to be granted a divorce. So you both will be free to remarry.

CHARLOTTE. No one but Edward has asked for my hand.

THE CAPTAIN. Charlotte —

CHARLOTTE. Do you remember that night, another life ago now, when the four us sat here — quiet and content? My dear friend, how far we have fallen. Edward and I wished to be alone in the country — so, I refused to adopt Ottilie. So, too, I refused to accept Edward's love for her — hoping it was infatuation or caprice — though I knew in my heart it was as strong and pure as *my love for you.* I was too proud, too stubborn — determined to believe that Edward and I were destined for one another. *I no longer believe in Destiny.* Only *chance.* Only pure … rich … irrational chance. *(She reaches out her hand to him, and he takes it.)* If Ottilie consents to marry Edward — *and only then* — will I agree to the divorce. And if then you'll have me, I will be your wife. The decision is hers alone. *(Music, and — distant thunder, as lights shift to —)*

The Rock Wall. Dusk.

Ottilie stands near the wall, holding the child. The wicker basket is on the ground, near her. After a moment, Edward appears, at a distance.

EDWARD. Tell me ... is it this wall — or this woman — which holds back the force of the water?

OTTILIE. *(Quietly, upon seeing him.)* I fear I'm looking at an apparition ...

EDWARD. No —

OTTILIE. I gave you up, Edward. I renounced you in exchange for your safe return.

EDWARD. And I am here —

OTTILIE. I had a premonition of your death. I saw you lying alone in a field. It filled me with such —

EDWARD. But, Ottilie, I am here — here in front of you. Our love has overcome death itself. *(He approaches, but does not touch her.)* We have, all of us, been tested these many months. And tonight our future shall be decided.

OTTILIE. *(Looking down at the child in her arms.)* Your future is here. *(Intermittent thunder is heard, as well as — the sound of a constant rain, as — Edward now views the child, his facing filled with tenderness, astonishment.)*

EDWARD. My God. He is remarkable. *(Aside.)* There, in his features, was the evidence of our crime. For he resembled not Charlotte and me — his true parents — but seemed, instead, the embodiment of the lovers we had imagined on that night. Our mutual deceit brought to life in the form of an angel.

OTTILIE. I want only your happiness, Edward. I can ask nothing more of you.

EDWARD. *(End aside.)* Yet, more can be granted. Even now, the Captain is asking Charlotte for her hand in marriage. And, with her consent, our own future shall begin.

OTTILIE. My love cannot abide deceit. Without Charlotte's blessing, I could never release my heart to you. *(Edward reaches his open hand out to her —)*

EDWARD. Believe me. It will all come to pass. *(Ottilie puts her hand in Edward's. He holds it, tightly, looking it ... then he kisses her hand. Note: This is the first time he has touched her in the play.)* We shall go to her. And learn of our fate. *(She wraps the blanket more tightly around the child —)*

OTTILIE. You must go alone.

EDWARD. But Ottilie —

OTTILIE. Please, Edward. I must insist. I cannot be at your side till she gives her consent.

EDWARD. *(Putting his coat around Ottilie's shoulders.)* Then, I will signal you from the estate. With the launch of a *single firework* — alighting the sky —

OTTILIE. That's not necessary —

EDWARD. *(Overlapping.)* — When you see that, you'll know that our future is assured!

OTTILIE. Go quickly, Edward. Before the storm begins —

EDWARD. You see, Fate does grant our desires — but must do so in its own fashion. How remarkable that is! *(Huge crack of thunder, as — the sounds of the storm — the wind, rain and thunder — build and are joined by — music, as — Edward rushes off, leaving — Ottilie, holding the child tightly, her back pressed against the rock wall, her eyes looking up to the sky. She is now lit only by moonlight amid the gathering dark. A shaft of light isolates Nick. He wears his contemporary clothes from the prologue. He is reading from the book.)*

NICK. *(Aside.)* "She had taken shelter at the rock wall, protecting the child from the wind and the rain. Never had the estate seen a storm of this kind." *(Separate shafts of light now gradually isolate — Charlotte, the Captain, and Edward.)*

CHARLOTTE. *(Aside.)* The Captain and I had just reached the pavilion when the sky opened.

THE CAPTAIN. *(Aside.)* We watched as the rain fell in sheets —

CHARLOTTE. Relentless and neverending —

THE CAPTAIN. Pounding the buildings and pouring down the hills —

NICK. "Until the tiny stream which emptied into the lake had become a *raging river.*"

EDWARD. *(Aside.)* I reached the estate and the rooms were empty.

CHARLOTTE. Where is Ottilie? Did she return?

EDWARD. CHARLOTTE!

THE CAPTAIN. I saw the water crashing against the dam —

NICK. "The swollen lake was now full to bursting — " *(The storm reaches a crescendo, as — Ottilie, desperate now, presses the full weight of her body against the rock wall —)*

CHARLOTTE. OTTILIE!

NICK. *"She presses her full weight against the dam —*

THE CAPTAIN. And I prayed to God it would hold —

NICK. "She is trying to hold back the raging water — the powers of man no match for the forces of nature — "

EDWARD. I ran outside just as — *(Huge crack of thunder/flash of lightning.)*

NICK. "At the last moment, she grabs the basket and places the child inside — " *(Ottilie places the child in the basket and holds the basket tightly, as the lights on her gradually isolate down to only a pinspot on her face.)*

EDWARD. OTTILIE! *(A terrible, destructive roar of water and land is heard, building —)*

NICK. "And no sooner has she done this, but *the rock wall begins to give way* — "

THE CAPTAIN. We heard a low moaning sound —

CHARLOTTE. And then a deafening roar which I will never forget —

NICK. "And the water rushes through, destroying the dam … and carrying Ottilie away." *Edward rushes out of the light, screaming —)*

EDWARD. NO!!! *(The roar rings hideously in the air, then a final sound of rushing water … and then, finally … silence. Ottilie's face alone remains lit, her eyes staring front, now calm, serene.)*

NICK. "Finally, in the hour before first light, two miracles are visited upon them: The Captain discovers the child's basket, floating in a field, far from the estate. The Captain wades into the water and as he takes hold of the basket — he hears a cry. The child is alive. *(The Captain is now holding the child in his arms. The Captain tears open his shirt and warms the child against his own chest — the first infant he has ever held; the greatest miracle he can imagine. A shaft of light discovers — Edward, at Ottilie's hope chest. During the following, he opens the chest ... and light pours up out of it and onto his face.)* And so, too, Edward — who feared he was to never again see Ottilie's face — discovers her that morning ... cradled in the limbs of a fallen poplar tree. Her skin cold and white. Her eyes wide open ... and looking to heaven.

CHARLOTTE. He tries to warm her. He throws his coat around her and presses himself to her — desperate to warm her — pleading with her to awaken ... *(Edward removes the chalice from his coat.)* His tears fall onto her lifeless cheeks and he mistakes them for her own. Hopeful now, he says her name and tightens his embrace. *(Edward removes the white dress from the chest, and wraps the chalice in the dress. He then places the chalice down inside the chest ... and, as he closes the lid ...)*

NICK. "But she is gone. Her body white as marble against the drifting, darkening lake. *(... The light on Ottilie goes to black.)* It is said that Edward never recovered from this sight."

CHARLOTTE. *(Quietly.)* We must forgive. And we must atone.

THE CAPTAIN. No attempt was made to rebuild the dam. In time, the once-flooded valley came back to life. And there in its center, weathered but indestructible ... was a bench. *(Music under, as — the Captain approaches Charlotte and places the child in her arms. Edward moves away from the hope chest, looking into the distance — his clothes now suggestive, once again, of those he wore in the Prologue.)* I did not return to my post in the city. Charlotte and Edward and I undertook a new life amid the shell of the old.

CHARLOTTE. There was, once again, no resentment, no bitterness between us. For there was, now, a child to raise.

THE CAPTAIN. We planted a stand of trees in Ottilie's memory.

CHARLOTTE. I saw to it that she was buried atop the hill she loved so dearly. In a crypt facing west.

THE CAPTAIN. And that night, Edward set off a single firework in her honor. It lit the sky for a too-brief moment ... then was gone. *(The Captain exits — walking past Nick, still reading.)*

CHARLOTTE. And only a few years later ... upon Edward's own death ... *(Charlotte walks up to Edward — and touches his face, gently.)* ... I buried him beside his beloved. That they who lost each other in this world, might find each other in the next. *(Charlotte turns and exits, walking directly past — Curt and Sharon, who enter with flutes of champagne, as the music fades, and lights expand to reveal —)*

EPILOGUE

A Park. The Present. Sunset.

Ed [formerly Edward] approaches Nick. Nick closes the book, turns to Ed, and — saying nothing — hands it to him. Nick goes, passing Curt and Sharon as they touch glasses and sip their champagne —

SHARON. Delicious. *(Mittler enters, packing up his camera, tripod, etc.)*

MITTLER. But how many of us ever find that person? That's my question.

CURT. *(With a laugh.)* Let it go, Mittler —

MITTLER. I agree with Ed — it's better not to think of what might have been. *(Curt and Sharon lift the picnic blanket and start off, calling to Ed.)*

CURT. C'mon — the others are waiting.

SHARON. If Ottilie arrives, tell her we're off to see the fireworks.

CURT. See you there! *(Curt and Sharon exit, together, as — Mittler follows them, then stops, turns to Ed.)*

MITTLER. I think I got a good one.

ED. Hmm?

MITTLER. This year's photo. One for the books. *(Mittler turns and exits. Ed is alone now, lost in thought, then — a young woman's voice is heard, calling —)*

OTTILIE'S VOICE. Are you there?

ED. Who's that? Hello? *(Lucy enters, barefoot and buoyant.)*

LUCY. Oh, I thought you were Nick. Have you seen him? The fireworks are about to start. *(Simply, from her heart.)* I really think I'm in love with him. Isn't that odd? And I wonder — does it always feel like this? Like no one could have possibly loved this way before? *(Ed stares at her ... then kindly brushes a strand of hair from her face. This gesture gives Lucy her answer. She smiles, and runs off, saying —)* See you there! *Adieu! (Ed is alone once again. He looks in the direction the others have gone. Then he looks down at the book in his hands. He sits ... and lifts the book ... and begins to read. Music begins, under, as — Ottilie appears, upstage. She now wears the simple, beautiful white dress from her hope chest. She looks around ... then slowly walks up directly behind Ed. He, of course, does not hear her approach. In the last, brilliant light of the day — Ottilie stands directly behind Ed — and begins to read over his shoulder. He remains unaware of her. Then ... after a moment ... Ottilie reaches out her hand and slowly turns the page of the book, as — Ed slowly turns his head and sees her. A final phrase of music, as — Ed and Ottilie look into each other's eyes, and — the lights fade to black.)*

End of Play

PROPERTY LIST

Wooden platform decorated with ribbons and flowers
Large rectangular stone covered with a large, brightly colored
    piece of fabric
Book (ED, NICK, OTTILIE, EDWARD)
Boom box (NICK, ED)
Frisbee, picnic blankets (LUCY)
Picnic basket (CHARLOTTE)
Backpack, small cooler with drinks (CAP)
Small wooden box with chalice (CHARLOTTE, MITTLER)
Camera on tripod (MITTLER)
Drink (MITTLER)
White parasol (SHARON, BARONESS)
Badminton rackets, bottle of champagne (CURT)
Letter (CHARLOTTE)
Map, small case of drafting and surveying equipment
    (CAPTAIN)
Pencil (CHARLOTTE, OTTILIE)
Letter (LUCIANNE)
Ledger, pencil (CHARLOTTE)
Scale model (CAPTAIN, EDWARD)
Tray with three cups of tea (OTTILIE)
Small object (CHARLOTTE)
Cup of tea (OTTILIE)

SOUND EFFECTS

Amplified camera click
Storm with thunder, rain, wind
Rain
Gurgling water
Fireworks
Two gunshots
Roar of dam bursting
Rushing water

NEW PLAYS

★ **SHEL'S SHORTS by Shel Silverstein.** Lauded poet, songwriter and author of children's books, the incomparable Shel Silverstein's short plays are deeply infused with the same wicked sense of humor that made him famous. "…[a] childlike honesty and twisted sense of humor." *–Boston Herald.* "…terse dialogue and an absurdity laced with a tang of dread give [*Shel's Shorts*] more than a trace of Samuel Beckett's comic existentialism." *–Boston Phoenix.* [flexible casting] ISBN: 0-8222-1897-6

★ **AN ADULT EVENING OF SHEL SILVERSTEIN by Shel Silverstein.** Welcome to the darkly comic world of Shel Silverstein, a world where nothing is as it seems and where the most innocent conversation can turn menacing in an instant. These ten imaginative plays vary widely in content, but the style is unmistakable. "…[*An Adult Evening*] shows off Silverstein's virtuosic gift for wordplay…[and] sends the audience out…with a clear appreciation of human nature as perverse and laughable." *–NY Times.* [flexible casting] ISBN: 0-8222-1873-9

★ **WHERE'S MY MONEY? by John Patrick Shanley.** A caustic and sardonic vivisection of the institution of marriage, laced with the author's inimitable razor-sharp wit. "…Shanley's gift for acid-laced one-liners and emotionally tumescent exchanges is certainly potent…" *–Variety.* "…lively, smart, occasionally scary and rich in reverse wisdom." *–NY Times.* [3M, 3W] ISBN: 0-8222-1865-8

★ **A FEW STOUT INDIVIDUALS by John Guare.** A wonderfully screwy comedy-drama that figures Ulysses S. Grant in the throes of writing his memoirs, surrounded by a cast of fantastical characters, including the Emperor and Empress of Japan, the opera star Adelina Patti and Mark Twain. "Guare's smarts, passion and creativity skyrocket to awesome heights…" *–Star Ledger.* "…precisely the kind of good new play that you might call an everyday miracle…every minute of it is fresh and newly alive…" *–Village Voice.* [10M, 3W] ISBN: 0-8222-1907-7

★ **BREATH, BOOM by Kia Corthron.** A look at fourteen years in the life of Prix, a Bronx native, from her ruthless girl-gang leadership at sixteen through her coming to maturity at thirty. "…vivid world, believable and eye-opening, a place worthy of a dramatic visit, where no one would want to live but many have to." *–NY Times.* "…rich with humor, terse vernacular strength and gritty detail…" *–Variety.* [1M, 9W] ISBN: 0-8222-1849-6

★ **THE LATE HENRY MOSS by Sam Shepard.** Two antagonistic brothers, Ray and Earl, are brought together after their father, Henry Moss, is found dead in his seedy New Mexico home in this classic Shepard tale. "…His singular gift has been for building mysteries out of the ordinary ingredients of American family life…" *–NY Times.* "…rich moments …Shepard finds gold." *–LA Times.* [7M, 1W] ISBN: 0-8222-1858-5

★ **THE CARPETBAGGER'S CHILDREN by Horton Foote.** One family's history spanning from the Civil War to WWII is recounted by three sisters in evocative, intertwining monologues. "…bittersweet music—[a] rhapsody of ambivalence…in its modest, garrulous way…theatrically daring." *–The New Yorker.* [3W] ISBN: 0-8222-1843-7

★ **THE NINA VARIATIONS by Steven Dietz.** In this funny, fierce and heartbreaking homage to *The Seagull*, Dietz puts Chekhov's star-crossed lovers in a room and doesn't let them out. "A perfect little jewel of a play…" *–Shepherdstown Chronicle.* "…a delightful revelation of a writer at play; and also an odd, haunting, moving theater piece of lingering beauty." *–Eastside Journal (Seattle).* [1M, 1W (flexible casting)] ISBN: 0-8222-1891-7

DRAMATISTS PLAY SERVICE, INC.
440 Park Avenue South, New York, NY 10016 212-683-8960 Fax 212-213-1539
postmaster@dramatists.com   www.dramatists.com